Jared Seide provides fail-safe practices which can transform you into a master of compassion. He speaks directly to the deep yearning of the human heart to connect with others and to join with their joys and suffering in ways that are helpful and life-giving. Cherish this book always — it will help to make you the person you have always wanted to be.

—Roshi Wendy Egyoku Nakao
Abbot Emeritus & Head Teacher
Zen Center of Los Angeles

I was introduced to the practice of Council as Inspector General for the California prison system. As Chairperson of the California Rehabilitation Oversight Board, I sought out innovative programs that might help improve our prison system and the men and women within it. I had the opportunity to view Council conducted within maximum security prisons with men serving life terms, and personally observed the emotional impact on them, some of whom had completely lost touch with their ability to feel. I also had other opportunities to develop my own mindfulness practice through my association with Jared and Council. So I have been privileged to reap the benefits personally and professionally. I now find myself in a new role as a Parole Commissioner who makes decisions regarding others' lives each day.

My own practice helps guide me and allows me to see and hear all those involved in the process; victims, the incarcerated, and those working within our criminal justice system. Not a week goes by when I am not reminded of Council's work in the prisons being life altering, either because of the change I can see and hear from inmates who have participated, and are now equipped to re-enter society, or by the unfortunate fact that many prisons still don't have the program available, and its absence is evident in the lack of emotional intelligence displayed by some inmates from those prisons. It is my hope that this book will help fill that gap. Improve a man's mind and he will hear better, improve a man's heart and he will listen better, improve both, and his soul will be better. Council has the capacity to do this, and Jared is one of the Soul-Changers.

—Robert Barton
Former Inspector General – Parole Commissioner
State of California

Starting with compassion and traversing the spaces of meaningful conversations -- precisely because they are uncomfortable and challenging -- Jared leads us through the structure of the council process and more significantly into the heart of listening to understand, learn, and attend to our humanity. This is mindfulness in practice offering hope across our differences and deep divides, a pathway which could not be more needed or opportune at this point in our communities and nation. This book is truly a gift for our times.

—John Paul Lederach
Professor Emeritus of International Peacebuilding
University of Notre Dame
Author of *The Moral Imagination: The Art and Soul of Building Peace*

This unique book comes at a critical time in our lives when the world needs each one of us to set aside our judgments, our language of "othering," and come together in the most meaningful way to achieve peace, respect, and compassion for self, for those we know, those we encounter, those we serve, and those we have yet to meet. Jared's remarkable expertise in bringing the practice of council to organizations, particularly those in the law enforcement arena, is, in my experience as a police chief, a key component in healing the rift between police and the communities they serve. What we have been doing has not worked. We need a new approach. Jared's book explains how to achieve this awareness, the ability to pay attention, and most importantly, without judgment of others.

This book is truly a gift to the world that will enable the reader to build the capacity to live a life of compassion in a skillful way that is beneficial to all. I firmly believe compassion is the gateway to achieving the desired outcomes and change that is desperately needed. I have personally experienced the power of the practice of council in settings that brought activists, police, clergy, and formerly incarcerated persons together resulting in deep authentic connections to each other, facilitating the capacity to perceive and experience each other through the lens of our shared humanity. How awesome would it be if we included this book in our police academies as a foundation for all other training. That is my hope.

—Jennifer Tejada
Chief of Police, Retired
Emeryville Police Department
Sausalito Police Department

Council calls us to experience "the other" through careful and attentive listening. The great sage Hillel implored, "If I am not for myself, who will be for me? And being only for myself, what am 'I'?" Jared Seide's new book, Where Compassion Begins, *launches each of us on a journey to truly be there for ourselves, so that we can truly prepare to be there for others.*

—Rabbi Yechiel Hoffman
US Director
Jewish Interactive

I am pleased to see the creation of Jared Seide's new book, Where Compassion Begins. *I'm confident this resource will act as a great supplement to the current curriculum and help others better understand the importance of mindfulness and other wisdom traditions. Jared Seide's work with Center for Council inside California's prisons has changed the lives of many.*

—Dr. Brant Choate
Director of Rehabilitative Programs
California Department of Corrections and Rehabilitation

Where Compassion Begins *is exactly what is needed now to bring the essence of compassionate communication more fully into the contemporary world. Jared Seide has woven together the practices of council and meditation in a personal and accessible way that support tangible life practices along the path of the heart,* Where Compassion Begins *is an imaginative bridge from the traditional roots of council and meditation to this moment in evolution, with contemporary references to science, medicine and recent understanding of the human condition.*

—Jack Zimmerman
Former Director of The Ojai Foundation
Author of The Way of Council

Where Compassion Begins

Where Compassion Begins

Foundational Practices
to Enhance Mindfulness, Attention
and Listening from the Heart

Jared Seide

Further information on the work of Center for Council may be obtained via its website, www.centerforcouncil.org, or by writing to: Center for Council, PO Box 292586, Los Angeles, CA, 90029.

DEDICATION

This is dedicated to the empty chair,

to those whose absence we bring into council,

to those whose shoulders we stand on

and to those who are longing to be in a circle, though they may not yet know it.

May this practice be of benefit, to us and to them all.

TABLE OF CONTENTS

Foreword

Greetings!

It's so good to meet you here. Thank you for taking the time to enter into the conversation that this book invites. This book has been created as a resource for those who have already had an opportunity to sit in a council circle, have attended a council training, or have practiced council for a while. Or maybe your curiosity has been ignited by a mention or recommendation and you are here to learn more. Either way, this book is intended for you, to begin, or to deepen your conversation with the practice of council as a skillful means of cultivating compassion. The hope is that you will soon find yourself in a circle with others—because council itself is the best teacher of council.

The word "council" derives from the Latin word *concilium*, which means "a coming together of people." This may seem like a simple definition—but that is council, at its core. Council offers us an invitation to bring our essential humanity into presence with others; we gather with an intention to offer regard and share our emerging story. Council does not require that we adhere to any particular belief system or spiritual path, it does not require expertise or background. The invitation is to come as you are and bring your best self, or the best you can do in the moment. Council is a place where all have a seat and everyone is valued. We take great care to create an inclusive circle and we remember what it means to speak and listen to one another with good intention and "from the heart."

Human interaction is often colored by judgment, agenda, analysis, opinion, bias and preference. But what if the practice of listening and speaking were offered without conditions? What if we felt the permission to say just exactly what was alive for us in the moment? What if we listened to one another with no need to agree, disagree, form an opinion, or have a stance? When we listen to the wind, we understand something about the weather, just as the sounds of the waves let us know something about the surf. We don't have to agree or disagree or have a position on it. The council circle is a way to contain and practice these simple intentions of speaking and listening from the heart with each other.

It's important to realize the value of the form—that is, how we organize and contain this gathering, the structure and limitations we agree to, and the intentionality we practice when we step into the council circle. To speak and listen from the heart asks of us something we may not be familiar with doing often: setting aside our agenda, judgment and opinions in order to listen attentively, with curiosity and regard. And to speak authentically, sharing what is true and real for us.

Each council is different, as the people who arrive are different versions of themselves every day, even if the membership of a given group does not change. Being present in council means that we allow ourselves to learn what the circle is in this very moment—and we give ourselves permission to share what we feel wants to be shared. When we leave the council circle, we take with us a deeper knowledge of the practice, of the group and, perhaps, of ourselves. I hope this book offers you a touchstone to return to, reminding you what we do when we come together in a council circle, as well as a chance to extend the lessons we learn in council into our lives outside of the circle.

—Jared Seide
Executive Director, Center for Council

Acknowledgements

It is an honor to hold the title of author of this book. I appreciate the opportunity to pull together a great deal of material, but I have no illusions that this material was anything I thought up. I am humbled by all that has gone into articulating these ways throughout the years and I hope these pages will do justice to the work of council and mindfulness and will provide further support and clarity as these practices continue to evolve.

I have had the great good fortune to have studied with and learned from many great teachers, mentors, allies and provocateurs and I have been graced with the collaboration of many more generous folks whose work this book celebrates. This book is the result of hard work and passion of the wonderful staff, interns and supporters of Center for Council, along with the many certified council trainers who live, study and share the practice of council in the world. We have learned so much together, as we have worked to bring this practice to a wide range of groups and individuals. I am grateful to our many allies, donors and funders, who have made possible the expansion of our programs and the creation of this book.

Most importantly, this book is the result of the wisdom, teachings, and lived experiences that have unfolded over the course of many years of practice. The work of mindfulness and council has roots that reach far and deep and the myriad brilliant and generous teachers who have helped to articulate much of what is documented here are far too many to name. Center for Council's lineage can be traced most recently through The Ojai Foundation, where scores of insightful visionaries, powerful wisdom keepers, devoted practitioners and passionate seekers convened, studied and codified practices that we now refer to as the Way of Council. Chief among these are the founder of The Ojai Foundation, Dr. Joan Halifax, and her two successors in leading that organization, authors of the book *The Way of Council*, Jack Zimmerman and Virginia Coyle. Jack has been my mentor and inspiration for many years and I am deeply indebted to him for his wisdom, love and care.

Teachers from many contemplative traditions have helped with the integration of council and mindfulness. It has been my great honor to have studied most extensively in the Zen tradition with Roshis Egyoku Nakao and Bernie Glassman; we are also most grateful to Dr. Jan Chozen Bays, for permission to integrate her work adapting mindfulness activities into the programs that Center for Council has developed for new audiences. On a personal note, I have had the great good fortune to bear witness to the ways in which council can nourish an intimate relationship, through the gift of my wife, council trainer and physician, Dr. Ann Seide. Ann has also been an enormous help in merging evidence-based scientific understanding of the autonomic nervous system and our bodies' response to stress with the contemplative aspects of council practice.

Center for Council is a continuation of all of these strands and exists in response to a profound longing for connection and presence. Our listening has led us to create council programs and trainings across many sectors. Since its founding in 2014, Center for Council has woven compassion-based practices into schools, businesses, nonprofit organizations, hospitals, law-enforcement agencies, faith-based communities, jails and prisons. We've also trained countless individuals to be council facilitators and have supported many recently certified council trainers along their paths. This book owes a great deal to all who have practiced council with us and who have helped to define, inspire and bring meaning to the practice.

We offer this book to you in the hope that it will honor all who have been called to this practice and who have helped define, embody and nurture it. As you read these words, you continue this great inquiry. May this book be a resource along your unfolding path.

How to Use This Book

This book is intended to be a resource to you in your exploration of the practice of council as a skillful means of cultivating compassion in your life and the world in which you live. It is divided into two sections.

The first section—*What is Council?*—includes explanations, definitions and distinctions that are part of the Introduction to the Way of Council Workshop. Once again, this book is not intended to teach you council, as much as to serve as a reminder of some of what is experienced in the council circle and taught in this introductory training workshop. The first part of the book includes definitions and explanations culled from many years of council practice in many settings.

The second section—*Deepening the Practice of Council: Seasons of Awareness*—includes material created to encourage you to extend the teachings of council into your life, outside of the council circle. You will find that the core intentions of listening and speaking from the heart can unfold in every facet of your life, well beyond the experience of the council circle. Indeed, like working out with weights, practicing council builds a kind of muscle, strengthening our ability to lead a meaningful, fruitful, compassionate life.

Some learn council in a weekend workshop led by certified trainers, others are introduced to council in their workplace, school, place of worship, or while incarcerated. Center for Council offers training in many forms, from the Council for Insight, Compassion & Resilience for incarcerated persons, to the Organizational Wellness Project for private and public businesses, to Compassion, Attunement, Resiliency Education (CARE) for healthcare providers, to Peace Officer Wellness, Empathy and Resilience (POWER) Training for police and correctional officers. All of these programs are built on the foundation of council and focus on developing self-awareness, strengthening communication skills and learning to practice compassion. The methodology of these programs remains consistent, although the format is adapted to each setting.

Both sections of this book are intended to provide you with resources to work with, as your practice deepens and evolves. We've also included some poems and quotations along the way to spur your imagination. We hope these resources will be of value when you are in a formal council group, as well as when you apply the tools you learn in council to informal interactions with friends, family and others. Formerly incarcerated folks have shared stories of utilizing the skills they learned in council at their parole hearings to great success. Many find that these new ways to think about speaking and listening from the heart have transformed relationships with their families and have been a critical part of navigating their reentry. Others who are introduced to the practice in their workplace seek us out to explore this work in more depth. Sometimes, it's an article or an email that prompts the introduction to a first experience in council—and a spark is ignited that leads to further inquiry and study. We are thrilled to offer workshops and trainings throughout the year to those who find their way to us and want to venture a little deeper.

Council has been introduced around the world, in diverse communities and in settings that vary from assisted living facilities to corporate board rooms, from schoolyards to surgical suites, from places of worship to government agencies. There's an enormous need for this work in all walks of life and those who have benefited directly from the practice are often great guides and teachers. We look forward to being with you in council and we're excited to learn of the ways you will carry this work into your next chapter.

PART ONE

WHAT IS COUNCIL?

We need to listen fully.
It's the basis of all compassionate action.
We need to listen not only to the voice of the person
who is hurting,
but to her bare feet,
the baby wrapped in her shawl,
and the stars in the cold night.
Such full listening helps us hear who is calling and what
we can do in response.
When we listen for the truth of the moment,
we know better what to do and what not to do,
when to act and when not to act.
We hear we are all here together,
and we are all we've got.

—Mirabai Bush
"Why Listening Is the Most Radical Act"

The ideals and democratic practices of the Iroquois Confederacy had a profound influence on Benjamin Franklin; he observed the Haudenosaunee people practicing talking circles and called these "councils," after the Latin word *consilium*. The essential practice of coming together in community has felt so nourishing for so many. When we set aside the noise and craziness of the fast-paced lives we live, quiet the distractions and chatter, and listen to our inner selves and each other, a kind of clarity and wisdom appears. In the early days of The Ojai Foundation, many elders and wisdom keepers from indigenous communities shared teachings around these ways and taught of the essential components and intentions. As this study intensified, Center for Council evolved as an initiative. The intention was to outline and codify a practice that would be the amalgam of many traditions and teachings, honoring the ancient sources from which these evolved, the generosity of diverse teachers who shared approaches and methods, and to adapt these practices for modern use. The process was detailed in a book called *The Way of Council*, written in 1996 and revised in 2009. Council programs were introduced in schools, nonprofit organizations and businesses, eventually landing in California Department of Corrections and Rehabilitation prisons in 2013. By that time, Center for Council had spun off to become an independent organization, committed to expanding the practice far and wide. Adaptations soon followed that enabled the organization to grow its core work in schools and organizations, as well as to create programs for healthcare professionals, law enforcement officers and government agencies.

As council programs expanded throughout communities, organizations and systems, the familiar appeal of what it means to be a tribe, a family, a fellowship resonated over and over. This desire to gather and celebrate community has been common in all cultures, but it has appeared in different forms, with different names. It has been called Ibitaramo in Rwanda, Ma'agal Hakshava in Hebrew traditions, Diwan and Loya Jurga in Islamic traditions, and a variety of other names in diverse cultures for many generations, as people have gathered in circles to deepen community. In all of these traditions, the practice of coming together with good intention has offered the opportunity to slow down and take a step away from the distractions and noise of daily life. When we focus on the present moment, we become more aware of all the possibilities for us to make active choices about the person we want to be and the community we want to create in our next chapter—a chapter that is unfolding around us with every breath. Council suggests we have agency in that unfolding. What if we really took responsibility for being the author of our story, for setting intentions around who we are to become? What if we could gather in council circles and initiate ourselves and each other into becoming the stewards of the next chapter of the human race?

To reflect like this on the big questions—and to really hear each other—we need a container. We need some way to hold these important conversations and encounters. We need a space in which it feels okay to be this vulnerable, to be this open, to imagine the world we want to create and leave behind to the next generations.

Council creates such a sturdy container, one that has the capacity to hold some very nourishing, often powerful, sometimes tender, moments of transformation.

Center for Council is deeply indebted to the generosity and insight of teachers and elders from a wide range of traditions and cultures who have shared teaching on how to create this kind of space and we are profoundly grateful for their care and partnership in helping to evolve and codify the practice of council for the institutions and systems in which we work today. Incorporating strands from many dialogic traditions throughout North America, and around the world, the way of council weaves these into a practice grounded in wisdom and presence and intended to be beneficial in our complex modern times.

Everywhere it is practiced, council holds the promise of reminding us of our true selves, demonstrating how much we have in common with everyone we encounter—even the most difficult—and showing us a vision of our limitless potential. The secret ingredient in this powerful, and sometimes mysterious, practice usually has something to do with compassion and how we come to understand what that word means to our own self-care, to the relationships we create with others and to the way we choose to walk in the world.

Guiding Principles

Council is a practice of open, heartfelt expression and attentive, empathic listening. Passing the talking piece with the intention of speaking authentically and listening attentively and without judgment inspires deeper communication, intercultural understanding and the nonviolent resolution of conflict. The regard of others in the circle offers the speaker encouragement to be honest and vulnerable, without fear of interruption or ridicule. Through deepening trust, council supports the clarification of values, co-visioning and community building.

Some general recommendations to keep in mind:

> Sit in a circle, on the same level—we're all in the same boat; no seat is better than another.
>
> Use a talking piece so that the speaker is known and recognized.
>
> Listen deeply, between the lines, to what is spoken—and to what is unspoken.
>
> Refrain from interruptions so as to respect the speaker; witness your internal responses and let them be until it's your time to speak.
>
> Speak honestly and from the heart.

Speak succinctly, aware of the time and group size.

Speak spontaneously, avoid rehearsing.

See each other as peers.

Share personal stories and truth, rather than positions and advice; avoid analysis and evaluation; there is no need to agree or disagree in council.

Seek a collective truth, viewpoint, wisdom—perhaps fuller than any one individual's truth.

Consider everything that enters the group's awareness as part of the process, including place, weather, who is there and not there, what has happened that day that has affected some or all of the participants, interruptions, and what's left unspoken in the silences.

Choose inquiry and questions over advocacy and speeches.

Choose curiosity over opinion.

Choose understanding over self-defense.

Choose building community over self-importance.

Choose being truthful over being right.

From the place where we are right
Flowers will never grow
In the spring.
The place where we are right
Is hard and trampled
Like a yard.
But doubts and loves

Dig up the world
Like a mole, a plow.
And a whisper will be heard in the place
Where the ruined
House once stood.

—Yehuda Amichai
"The Place Where We Are Right"

The Five Basic Elements
of Council

Every council takes into consideration five basic structural elements, whether obvious or inferred.

1) *The Circle*

The shape of the circle itself creates a sense of equality. We can see everyone who is present. All seats are equally important. There is no beginning or end. We face each other. We remember that, together, we make up something more than the sum of the parts. Even when virtual, the essential qualities of circle can be evoked creatively.

2) *The Center*

Every circle has a center; we can make that center meaningful. The center actually and symbolically holds common intentions and values. It is the heart of the circle and it can be represented by objects of significance, or by things that are spoken in the center in the form of a "dedication" of the council to something meaningful, generous, precious, and true for the speaker. The commonality of the group is represented, along with the intent to honor the greater whole. Objects in the center can be picked up and held, unless that is logistically impossible; in online councils, we can symbolically honor what is in our center and imagine a talking piece being passed from one speaker to the next. The *talking piece* chosen becomes a tool for focusing attention and for empowering the one holding it, on behalf of everyone there.

3) *Marking the Beginning, or Creating the Threshold*

An intentional opening indicates that we are about to do something set apart from our usual ways of being together; we step into this together. It may be helpful to pause and make sure everyone is ready and aware that the council is to begin and then to step in deliberately. Nobody should stumble, or be dragged into council, or feel forced to participate. Everyone entering council should be ready and step in willingly.

4) *The Four Intentions*

The root meaning of the word *intend* is *stretch*. Unlike a rule, an intention is something we make up our minds to try our best to do, but we are also aware that it may be very difficult to achieve. Council is considered a practice and it is important to make a commitment to practice the intentions when stepping into council:

Listen from the heart

Set aside the tendency to judge, analyze or form opinions and try to listen with curiosity and openness to what is said in order to understand.

Speak from the heart

Set aside agenda, plans, or what you think you should say and try to speak what is alive and true in this very moment.

Be spontaneous

Set aside what you have been preparing or rehearsing and try to speak what is coming up for you right now.

Be lean

Set aside the full context and all the many details and try to focus on the essence of what is coming up for you, just what is needed to be said and no more.

5) *Marking The Close, or Stepping Away*

Note the end of this time and mark the transition out of council in a good way. It is often good to celebrate the council or express some gratitude and appreciation, if appropriate, for both the honest and courageous storytelling and for the attentive and respectful listening. When participants step out of council, they make an agreement with one another to close the circle and hold all that was said as sacred and confidential. If the confidence is broken and stories are re-shared outside of council, it will erode the strength of the container. Confidentiality builds safety and trust and our agreements to keep confidence begin upon ending the council. That said, no one person can guarantee confidentiality, it must be honored and embodied by all who participate, so that the council container will feel reliable and strong.

Pointers on Listening from the Heart

The most basic and powerful way to connect to another person is to listen. Just listen. Perhaps the most important thing we give each other is our attention.... A loving silence often has far more power to heal and to connect than the most well-intentioned words.

—Rachel Naomi Remen
Kitchen Table Wisdom: Stories That Heal

When practicing the intention of listening from the heart, keep these things in mind:

Seek understanding instead of agreement.

Accept others as they are instead of trying to fix them.

Empathize instead of criticizing or judging.

Read the field, the group energy and the mood of the circle.

Stay centered and focused on the speaker, resist distraction.

Stay present in the stories, instead of mind-wandering or avoiding.

Notice your internal responses, but don't get caught up in them.

Honor feelings, your own and those of others.

Look for the bigger story, the unspoken narrative.

Listen for the voice of the circle, the themes that may be emerging for
the group.

Practice not agreeing or disagreeing *on any level*, just listen to understand.

Pointers on Speaking
from the Heart

Tell me a fact and I'll learn.

Tell me the truth and I'll believe.

But tell me a story and it will live in my heart forever.

—Native American proverb

When practicing the intention of speaking from the heart, keep these things in mind:

Use "I" statements instead of "you" or "we" to avoid characterizing others' thoughts or feelings.

Tell your personal story instead of philosophizing.

Favor feelings over facts and opinions.

Reveal your process, "how I got where I am," and your conclusions.

Move toward vulnerability, instead of away from it.

Tell the fullest possible truth, instead of edited truths.

Share spontaneously instead of rehearsing or editing.

Speak leanly; cut to the chase; avoid fill or "thinking out loud."

Key Components
and Definitions

You have noticed
that everything an Indian does is in a circle,
and that is because the Power of the World
always works in Circles,
and everything tries to be round,
and I have heard this earth is round like a ball,
and so are the stars.
The wind in the greatest, whirls.
Birds make their nests in circles,
for theirs is the same religion as ours...
Even the seasons form a great circle in their changing,
and always come back to where they were.
The life of man is a circle
from childhood,
and so it is in everything
where the power moves.

—Black Elk, Oglala Sioux Holy Man
Black Elk Speaks

Creating the Container

Make the physical space intentional, harmonious, and inviting before council begins.

Arrange seating in a circle, unless that is absolutely impossible.

Try to have a clear space, without tables, desks, or other furniture in the middle of the circle that might create a barrier.

Honor the center of the circle with symbols and objects meaningful to the group.

As much as possible, try to avoid interruptions.

Openings

Invite any clearings or important announcements that may need to be offered before council begins.

Honor the transition into council with a moment of silence or centering, mindful breathing, someone offering a poem or a song, or asking, "are we ready to go into council?"

Consider a check-in or brief *speed round* to bring people together and open the space for deeper issues to surface.

Talking Piece

The talking piece is a physical object that:

focuses the attention of participants on the speaker;

signals a clear beginning and ending to each person's sharing, by passing along;

assures that each speaker has full time to complete the share and gets to decide when it is done;

creates a pause or beat between speakers, during which the group can digest what has just been said;

identifies the next speaker;

can always be held in silence, or just passed; and

represents, when at rest in the center of the circle, the heart of council and community.

The Facilitator

The facilitator (from the Latin word *facilitare*, meaning to make easy):

establishes and clarifies the intentions and ground rules before beginning council;

assists the circle in clarifying its needs regarding goals and logistics, including confidentiality, timeframes, breaks, ending;

safeguards the integrity of the council process and the container;

reads the field and encourages the flow of group energy;

redirects any focus and/or attention to the circle and the center;

invites any voice or perspective that may be missing;

when in doubt as to what to do next, asks the group; and

whenever possible, pairs with a co-facilitator.

Witnessing

Witnessing is offered at the end of a council session in the form of a coun-

cil round or popcorn, or offered to one or more members, or if there
is time, a brief word from everyone.

Witnessing confirms that voices have been heard and allows the group to
experience and celebrate its collective wisdom.

Witness comments can be invited to reflect on the process of the council,
the words and content shared, or the responses that emerged.

Witnessing can be an opportunity for recalling and sharing literal and/
or conceptual echoes and resonances of stories that were shared—
not participants' opinions of things said; try to avoid "I liked it when
somebody said…" or "I disagree with something that was said…."

The Witness-Participant

The witness-participant is a member of the council who:

usually remains silent throughout the council, sharing at the end, after all
participants have finished, offering the last word;

listens for what the overarching council is creating, embraces the heart of
the group, honors its highest intention, moves toward the emerging
"voice of the circle;"

maintains relatively unbiased perspective, holds an eagle's eye view of
what the group is engaged in, not favoring any one seat or voice; and

when invited, may offer feedback on the group's process and dynamics, or
on content and subject matter of the council—or may remain a
"silent witness."

Turning Into The Skid

When circumstances or a sudden eruption of suppressed issues, feelings, or prob-
lems take over and derail the planned agenda, *go with it*. If possible, the facilitator

should not deny or pretend this isn't happening. Instead, embrace the disruption, and lead the group toward the learning or opportunity that may be hiding within the chaos, leaning into the intentions and forms of council. This is known as turning into the skid, a phrase which is derived from the instruction offered to operators of rear-wheel drive vehicles as the best way to avoid an accident when about to skid out of control. Facilitators should develop comfort with and model this skill, but it may be initiated or practiced by any participants. It may be as simple as naming something "hot" that has come up and noting one's internal response when witnessing, or it may require the facilitator shifting the form of the council or adjusting the planned prompts to move in a new direction.

Reading The Field

The practice of council calls for the deepest of listening. This includes listening for the collective voice of the circle. We speak of this as reading the field. This field, or group voice, is not simply the sum of the moods and energies of each individual, but rather the synergy of our joined hearts and minds. It is something entirely new and unique in the moment for each council circle. In practical terms, reading the field means being aware of the mood and energy, the needs, intentions and overall progress of the circle as a whole, even as we are speaking ourselves or listening to others. We attune to the content of what is said, the feeling tone of the council, the physical movements of participants and the energetic sense of the unspoken. We may even develop a sense of "where this is going." A reminder can be found in the first letters (F.I.E.L.D.):

> Feelings
>
> Intentions
>
> Energy
>
> Language (verbal and body)
>
> Destiny (where the conversation is headed)

This is *not* a call to analyze (or, worse, to psychoanalyze) the group individually or collectively, but an invitation simply to be aware of the ebbs and flows of the group's field, along with everything else. The practice of paying attention to the *field* is the essence of *witnessing.* It is a challenge specific to council to be both participant and witness simultaneously, sharing *who I am* in the context of *who we are becoming.* Whether we are conscious of this or not, this field exerts a powerful force on what we think, feel, sense and on the choices we make, large and small. The more aware we can be of the voice of our emerging community, the more compassionate and effective we become as facilitators and stewards, supporting the unfolding, but not trying to shape it.

Closings

The facilitator is responsible for keeping track of time and navigating to a closing, staying aware of the remaining time allotted and agreed to, so as not to create a jarring finish to the council. Reading the group field, the facilitator should determine the group's needs regarding closure, such as a short speed round, a moment of silence, an expression of gratitude or celebration, a discussion of next steps after the council is closed. If there is time and it serves, there may be an opportunity for anyone or everyone to offer a closing witness comment—perhaps one brief final round, or placing the talking piece in the center for participants to use in adding an afterthought, or noting that "there are two minutes left for a closing word or two from anyone who wants," for example. Invite any witness-participants to share at this time. Always end with a formal or ceremonial gesture—a group movement, a thank you, a cheer, a moment of silence, a wave, "passing the pulse" or a stomp pattern, whatever might be appropriate to mark a clear ending to the intentional time in council and a stepping-back into the world outside of council. This clear, enacted ending piece is critical for marking completion of the council and closure of this unique time together. The group deliberately steps away from the experience together, moving back into the "real world" where intentions and interactions may be quite different and our vulnerability and interpersonal commitments may have to shift.

Basic Formats
for Council Circles

Basic Council

When using the basic form of council, the talking piece passes around the circle in an agreed-upon pattern (usually clockwise). This form of council is ideal for assuring that everyone who wants to may speak; it is good for opening and closing group processes and for assessing the group voice. This form may be used for an open council or a council focused on a particular theme. When the talking piece then moves in a different direction (say, counter-clockwise), that may mark a departure from the group's usual routine.

Popcorn

The talking piece sits in the middle; the speaker picks up the piece when moved to do so, returning it to the center after talking, and so on. This is the council form of dialogue—good for discovering themes, weaving images, developing the group story or going deeply into specific issues.

Web

The talking piece is tossed by the speaker to someone else in the circle, determined by a gesture that the new speaker makes or by the choice of the speaker—remembering that anyone can pass at any time and nobody is ever compelled to speak.

Fish Bowl

Two or more seats form a center circle. People are chosen or choose to be in those seats and the talking piece is passed around, or offered popcorn style; afterwards, the talking piece may be passed to the outer circle, which may pass it around and offer witness comments. Sometimes useful when there are different subgroups within a group (gender, age group, organizational roles). Good for unpacking hot issues, understanding internal divisions and encouraging team or group feedback.

Spiral

Three or more seats in the inner circle; volunteers flow from outer to inner circle, and back again; each turn involves both speaking and listening. The inner seat-taker listens to the person following their share before returning to the outer circle. Develops spirit of inquiry within a group, taps energy around an issue and may be useful for conflict exploration/resolution.

Response Council

The person holding the talking piece may empower brief dialogue with other people, short responses to questions, or improvisational moments, all while still holding the talking piece, within the single turn to speak. A person might choose to explore something in a deeper way by holding the talking piece and asking for input or response from as many people as desired—from one person to the entire circle. The response council ends when the holder passes the talking piece.

Dyadic Council

Two people sit in council and pass the piece between them, exploring an issue, developing a vision, etc. One or more "witnesses" may be present, within or outside the pair and may offer their comments and perspectives, either during or at the end of the process as pre-arranged. The dyad may set a third seat to represent the essence of the relationship, the "Third Presence," the bigger picture. Participants or witnesses may move to the third seat to speak from that perspective. (This practice is often used by intimate couples to explore their relationship and is explained in more detail in the book *Flesh and Spirit: The Mystery of Intimate Relationship*, by Jack Zimmerman and Jaquelyn McCandless.)

Forming Council Prompts

Forming an effective prompt is part of the council facilitator's art and mastering this takes time. While topics should be of interest or relevant to the whole group, a good prompt must be one that participants feel they *can* respond to and one that they *will* respond to—something that prompts a story.

Although council topics can involve participants in reflections upon the past, expressions in the present, and views of the future, most often we begin by asking them to recall actual experiences related to the topic. For example, if the topic were "fun," a good prompt would be: "recall a time when you found yourself thinking, 'wow, this is *really* fun!'" You can add, "wait for the talking piece to come, and then see what story comes to you." Sometimes it's good to preface the prompt with an example of your own, or with a discussion of the key term. The facilitator's share then serves as a chance to model one possible response to the prompt. Alternatively, the facilitator may also choose to pass the talking piece to someone else to start or ask if anyone in the circle would like to start.

A good way to articulate a prompt may begin with, "tell about a time when..." or "share a story of a time when..." or "recall an experience when...." instead of, "what do you think about...," which might lead to analysis or intellectualizing.

To develop a council about dealing with stress, the prompt, "tell a story about a time you had to deal with stress" is probably a more effective prompt than, "why is it important to deal with stress?" Good prompts invite personal stories, not theories or opinions.

Remember that a prompt is not so much a question to be answered as it is an invitation to begin a reflection, to explore one's response—beyond inviting a simple "answer to the question." Also, remember that speaking from the heart always takes precedence over speaking to the topic. Therefore, after offering a question or prompt it is a good practice to add "or anything else you wish to say!" Sometimes a participant may take the prompt in an unexpected direction, which is a great opportunity to expand the resonance of the topic.

Forming council prompts takes practice! Start with your own experiences and trust the process.

Remember, effective council prompts are always:

> stated in the clearest possible terms;
>
> of interest to the facilitator (don't exclude yourself);
>
> relevant to the whole group (know who is in the circle);
>
> appropriate and not offensive; and
>
> free from assumptions, opinions, or unchecked value judgments.

Also, good prompts:

> invite the group to move beneath theories or opinions and enable each member to access and share from experience, rather than what we "think" or what we "know;"
>
> are not requests to "share feelings;" feelings often emerge when we share experiences, but "how did you feel when..." is not an effective invitation to tell a story; trust the speaker to go as deep as he or she wants to go and to share what feels right for him or her;

allow for the entire spectrum of human response; avoid leading questions that guide participants to look at only a few responses to an experience; if the topic is "loneliness," it is better to offer "talk about a time when you were lonely," rather than "talk about a time you were overwhelmed by terrible loneliness and you handled it really badly;" and

explore and invite consideration of the prompt and the stories that unfold; some shares may address the prompt directly, others peripherally, or perhaps in an entirely unexpected way; a prompt should come with permission to go wherever the speaker wants or needs to go; consider adding "...or anything else" to the end of the prompt; avoid asking for agreement or critique, pushing people to "go deep" or making veiled statements of opinion.

Effective and appropriate prompts are different for every circle, every time. A facilitator who tries to push a prompt on a group that does not fit with the mood or energy that the group is experiencing can create a very negative experience. Even a well-constructed prompt—or a prompt that made great sense earlier—may be the wrong prompt for the moment. That said, what follows are some examples of prompts that have been effective in past circumstances.

To Get Acquainted or Break the Ice

Tell a story about your name. Are you named after someone—what do you know about the person? Does your name have special meaning? Does your name fit you? Have you ever considered changing your name—or done so?

Are you the oldest, youngest, middle or only child? Tell a story about how that is for you.

When a holiday is approaching: What traditions did you grow up with at this time of year? Tell a story about a memorable moment that happened during this season.

To Explore Listening

How do we know when someone is really listening to us? What are some clues that suggest they are *not* listening?

What person in your life is an excellent listener? How do you know? Tell a story about a time when someone really heard you.

Tell about a time when you felt really listened to, seen in your fullest potential, or a time when you did not feel seen, or felt invisible. Talk about a time when you truly listened to someone else, or did not.

To Explore Friendship

When did you know someone was going to be a good friend? What qualities did you observe?

Without naming names, talk about how you met one of your closest friends. Did you know instantly that you would be friends, or did it take a while?

Tell a story about a time you knew that a friend really had your back—or you had the back of one of your friends. Tell about a time when a friend let you down—or you let down a friend.

To Explore Life's Adventures

Tell a story about a time you did something daring.

Tell a story about an extreme experience you have had with one of the four elements (water, fire, earth, air).

Complete this sentence: "I have been happiest when I am..." Doing what? And where?

Meditation and Council

Feelings come and go,
like clouds in a windy sky.
Conscious breathing is my anchor.

—Thích Nhat Hanh

Meditation provides us with a formal practice of coming to a stop, settling our-
selves so that we are able to notice what's really going on inside of us and around
us. It is an opportunity to fully experience the present moment, but it requires
that we hone our ability to focus our attention and to let go of the thoughts
and internal chatter that is often in the background, distracting us. Meditation
provides us with a practice that we can pick up to become an expert student of
ourselves and the environment in which we live. It's a practice that can be founda-
tional as we journey into greater mindfulness and embodying the way of council.

The more we come to be an astute witness of the present moment, the more
we understand the process of change, how everything changes, and how this
moment passes into the next. This can reinforce the way in which we show up
in council, and in our lives. Meditation does not equate to religion—there is no

belief system to take on, or to reject. It is really a practice of paying attention to what is here in the moment and what is arising. It requires that we resist the urge to judge or reject anything, so as to stay attentive to the present moment. Meditation also helps us develop the capacity to *respond* rather than *react* by creating a little space between having an experience, and what we habitually do in response to that experience.

Meditation offers us the opportunity to be still and concentrated, which is an important quality in our ability to practice council. Developing a meditation practice builds our capacity to witness and listen more thoroughly to that which is unfolding around us. Meditation requires that we first settle the body, then settle our attention; focusing on our breath can be a great way to settle ourselves. As we breathe in, usually without any thought or planning, our body takes in the oxygen it needs to survive in the next few moments. When we exhale, we let go of things that our body no longer needs. Somehow, this happens over and over again, throughout our days, throughout our lives. It does not require that we do anything, it just happens. This phenomenon of breathing is always available as a focal point, offering us an ever-present opportunity to focus our attention on something that is happening all the time.

Meditation hones our focus on this very moment of our existence. The capacity to reside in the present moment can be a powerful shift from getting stuck in either replaying the past or fantasizing about the future. We realize that there is really nothing we can do to change the past and, as much as we might try, we cannot control what will happen in the future. Things that have caused us pain or shame or regret can only be addressed in the here and now. Likewise, feelings of dread or fear of the future have no value to us, we can only adjust our present experience to support the emergence of a good outcome. Meditation builds our capacity to reside in the present moment, right now, where we can have a real impact on who we are and who we are becoming.

Every contemplative tradition has an approach to meditation—and the study of this practice can be very beneficial. You may encounter teachings on mindfulness, breath work, Zen meditation (zazen or shikantaza), body scans and progressive muscle relaxation, guided imagery and loving kindness meditations, qigong and yoga, centering prayer, and so on. All of these provide a pathway to explore meditation; find one that is right for you. While meditation may occur before a council session, it can also be something you choose to do wherever you are. You can sit on a chair, or the floor, or a bed; you can even meditate while walking.

Here's one simple method you might try to get started:

> Take some time to find a comfortable seated position.
>
> Bring some attention and dignity to your posture.
>
> Settle your body, and then settle your attention on one spot in front of you, give yourself some time for that.
>
> Become aware of your breath and observe the sensations as air moves in and out; notice the place air enters and leaves your body, where it goes and how your body adjusts.
>
> As you watch your breath, make sure you are in a position that enables you to breathe in and out comfortably.
>
> Notice the sensations inside your body and immediately around you, the sounds, the light, distractions—and bring your attention back to the breath, allowing yourself to observe it without the need to control it.

Make a plan to do this for 5 minutes, 15 minutes, or perhaps building to 30 minutes at a time.

Know that you will be distracted, especially if you meditate for a long period of time. That is completely natural. You always have the ability to come back to the breath, to bring your attention back and allow it to rest on that miracle of your body breathing out and breathing in. Just observe that. You can view each distraction as another opportunity to catch your attention and bring it back to your breath kindly, the way you might redirect an eager puppy. It is in that moment when you notice your attention has strayed, and you gently bring attention back to the breath, that you build the muscle of meditative attention.

Meditation offers a break from the constant thought-stream in your mind and creates the ability to hit the pause button and take in what is actually there. We can't stop our thinking and meditation is not intended to do that. It just offers us the chance to focus where our attention is pointed. In essence, council itself is its own type of meditation, some call it "a group mindfulness practice," as we are asked to focus completely on what is being shared by each participant and nothing else. Some council groups encourage participants to bring in their own type of meditation and offer it to the group as part of the "settling down" that occurs before a dedication and the beginning of passing the talking piece and sharing. As you find your own relationship to a practice of focusing your attention and concentration, the connection between this practice of mindful attention and your experiences embodying council in your group and in your life will become more obvious. You will find that meditation and council are practices that complement and strengthen one another.

The term "mindfulness" has become a popular expression and it is a general term that refers to practices that give us an opportunity to slow down and turn our attention toward what we are experiencing in each unfolding moment of our lives. Jon Kabat-Zinn, the founder of Mindfulness-Based Stress Reduction, defines mindfulness as "awareness that arises through paying attention, on purpose, in the present moment, non-judgmentally." The concept of non-judgment is very much connected to the intention of listening from the heart in council. It is an approach that enables us to really engage in what we are experiencing, bringing our full attention to the moment, so that we may understand, discern and take action deliberately, with intention. Practicing mindfulness, we become the authors of the story of our lives, the architects of our next chapter. This empowerment is something we find together when we gather in council, but it's also available to us in every moment of our lives, as the second half of this book will explore. Living mindfully and engaging in a group practice like council are powerful ways to take responsibility for the life we want to lead and the world we want to create for ourselves and for generations to come.

Worldwide Cultural Dialogic Practices

Our survival as a species depends on our ability to recognize that our well-being and the well-being of others are in fact one and the same.

—Marshall B. Rosenberg

The practice of council owes a great debt to teachers and wisdom holders from a variety of traditions and cultures who have generously shared insight, experiences and applications that have evolved over many generations from around the world and have inspired and been incorporated into the methodology of council. You are encouraged to explore the roots of these practices.

Some dialogic practices from other cultures that are congruent and share much with the practice of council include:

Native American: Haudenosaunee Council, Lakota Hocokah, diverse traditions of Talking Circle, Healing Circle, Peacemaking Circle

Hawaiian: Ho'oponopono

African: Daré (Zimbabwe); Ibitaramo (Rwanda); Fambul Tok (Sierra Leone)

Australian Aboriginal: Initiation Ceremonies

Finnish: Kehrä

Tongan: Faikava

Samoan: Su'ifefiloi

Southern Venezuela/Northern Brazil (Yanomami Tribe): Wayamou

Jewish: Havurah, Hevreh (Ma'agal Hakshava), Farbrengen (storytelling gatherings)

Christian: Listening Circles; Cursillo, Quaker Friends Meetings, Devout Listening and Hearing "The Call"

Islamic: Sobhet, Diwan, Loya Jurga

Old Slavic: Veche

Hindu: Satsang

Social Psychology and Mathematics: Kurt Lewin's Field Theory

Psychology and Anthropology: Marshall Rosenberg's Nonviolent Communication, Narrative Therapy, Arnold van Gennep, Victor Turner

Organizational Management: MIT Dialogue Project, Theory U, Presencing Institute,

Society for Organizational Learning

Scientific Humanism: Bohm Dialogues

Judicial Practice: Restorative Justice Circles, Community Conferencing Circles, Tribal Law, Gicaca Court (Rwanda)

Literacy: Paolo Friere's "Investigative Circles," Miles Horton's Highlander

Folk School

Education: William Glasser's "Classroom Meetings," Waldorf Education's Goethean Conversations; Collaborative for Academic, Social and Emotional Learning (CASEL)

Literary References: *The Iliad, The Jungle Book, Lord of the Rings, Touching Spirit Bear, etc.*

A Thought Experiment

As you consider the image below, note what you see first, describe it to yourself. As you do, see if there is another way to perceive and understand the picture you are examining.

This is a famous image entitled "My Wife and My Mother-in-Law." It's an optical illusion depicting both a young woman turning away and the profile of an older woman (the younger woman's necklace is also the older woman's mouth). Some see both images easily, yet others have a hard time letting go of what they think they are seeing and cannot see the second woman's image. It's a good example of how our ability to really take something in has a lot to do with our willingness to catch ourselves in our assumptions and let go of what we think we're going to encounter in order to see what's there.

Sometimes the superficial image we have of someone, or the judgment we bring, or the bias we carry, can diminish our ability to really see that person fully— or even to listen well to what they have to say. Our ability to take in what we encounter increases greatly when we let go of assumptions—what we think we know, what we've been conditioned or taught to see, what we are expecting; we give ourselves a chance to better understand what's there when we let go of these assumptions. When we train ourselves to slow down, pay attention, resist reactivity, and expand our awareness, we build our capacity to reside in the present moment and to make deliberate, positive choices about what we want to do and who we want to be, based on what's really in front of us.

The next section of this book is intended to encourage your practice, in and out of the council circle. There are infinite opportunities to pay attention and make good decisions about how our path will unfold. As we build more opportunities for council to emerge in institutions, organizations and communities, we can also find ways to fine-tune our individual capacity for awareness and compassion, noticing how we show up, developing greater insight into ourselves and the world around us and making good choices about how we step into our next chapter.

Faces and Voices of Council

Anna Maria, arts organization leader

"We basically started a practice of council in our organization and it's transformed the way we create artistic work."

Carey, prison administrator

"Literally, within the first day, four of these big old tough guys were in tears, sharing their heart... it was an amazing thing to see... I track their 'disciplinaries' and... I've seen a huge transformation and I can truly tell you that these guys, they have been successful, they are staying out of trouble and they are opening their eyes to new ways of thinking... I've been very impressed. I'm so happy the program is here and we're proud to have it."

Edward, incarcerated in state prison (granted parole)

"Council has pushed me. It's been healing for me. It actually got me to communicate, it actually helped me to open up more, it actually helped me learn how to empathize with other people and see things from other points of view... When you're opening up to other people, and they're listening to you, and you have the opportunity to express yourself without being judged and criticized, you hear the commonality and it helps you. Council helps you learn to discover the true you, that part of you that God created, who you really are: someone who is loving, caring, compassionate, that's what the human spirit is and that's what Council has helped me bring out."

Gena, police lieutenant

"As you sit around the circle and you hear the history of what the council is all about, it makes you see the similarities among each other and how uniquely wonderful we are as the human race. Regardless of your background, or if you've been in prison, or if you're a cop, or if you're an attorney, or if you're just a regular old mom. There are shootings and murders and robberies and children are being harmed; that seeps into your spirit. You don't just walk away from a homicide, you don't walk away from seeing somebody's life being taken... that stays real in your mind. How do you take care of yourself when those things happen? Self-care, meditating, and getting in a council and talking about it, and debriefing, and sharing... it's therapeutic. Everyone said it made them a better husband, a better father, a better partner..."

James, incarcerated in state prison (granted parole)

"I was hooked the first time. I'm a lifer and I continue to get a lot of growth out of Center for Council. Council is all about developing skill sets to live an ethical life and to express humility and kindness to other people as well as being able to work on self-esteem and self-dignity. Council allows us to go deep into areas of our life that we never thought would be possible; it's a way to heal the shame that has bound us up and kept us from being our true self. Center for Council allows us to feel like we're human beings, not just inmates...Center for Council creates a ripple effect of personal growth."

Joseph, incarcerated in state prison

"What I found with Center for Council was something totally unexpected. I started to recognize a need for a change in me, a need to give back. I wasn't seeing people as who they were, I was only thinking of me, what can they do for me... and that way of thinking got me to prison. I thought, what can I do to change that? I've been taking, taking, taking... how do I flip that? What Center for Council has helped me to see is that I can give back, that I have something valuable to offer that I didn't realize I had."

Mitch, incarcerated in state prison (granted parole)

"I've been in pretty much every group in this prison and this one is different. Being in this group, I learned how to feel someone's story, someone's pain. It's broken stereotypes and the usual way inmates view people who look different. This has almost re-sensitized me to be more human again. I used to have a lot of false strength, I was very selfish before and... it's humanized me. I truly, genuinely care about the next man. Council helped me develop a sense of trust and has helped me empathize and gain insight into my childhood. It put me in a place where I could be vulnerable inside a place you're not supposed to be. I'm forever thankful for it. It's truly helped me on my path."

Patti, nonprofit organization leader

"We use council in many different circumstances. I think it's a process that's quite adaptable. It's a way to come together as a community. Council really is a practice of authenticity. We use it with our volunteers, we use it with our youth, we use it with our staff, and listening is one of the most important things that we train on. This enables people to come together to listen in community. What council does is help that integration and that reconnection happen again. Council is a miracle skill."

Randolf, prison warden

"I think any time you talk in such a manner where you can listen and know that you're listened to, and appreciate and understand each other a little more, I think your chances for resolve are much higher. And I think that's what council does.... If you can impact a level four maximum security prison, you have no excuse, you can impact a city or a county, or if you want to go on a macro level, you know, a world..."

Sam, formerly incarcerated in state prison

"It brought me to a place in my life where I was able to explore my crime and the impact that my actions had on my victims, my community, and my family. And as I put myself in the shoes of all the people that my choices had affected, I began to change my attitude and the trajectory of my life... moving away from the destruction and violence and toward peace and healing. The more we can get council to the prison population, the more we can decrease violence and racial tensions on the prison yards. Council is about building community and working toward healing, as we come to understand each other and see that we all have similar stories. I no longer saw other inmates through the lens of the gang, as the enemy; I saw them as someone waiting to be heard, listened to, understood with compassion and empathy, potential links in this chain of peace and human-kindness."

Shawn, police lieutenant

"We see ourselves as indestructible, we're always the ones called by people in need and we always respond but who's there when we need it? I think the more people we have understanding that it's okay to be vulnerable, it's okay to know that you're not indestructible, the better. If you have that ability in the small council huddles of saying, "you know what, I got a story to tell you," then you know you're not alone. I think it's gonna help many, and I think it's going to change a lot of dispositions and it's going to soften that hard outer shell that we all as police officers develop over time, whether we realize it or not. It makes us more understanding. I think it makes us wiser. It gives us that ability to be organic. And we're human, we're not made of steel."

Sofia, activist and facilitator

"Being in council is so much about noticing what you notice and just listening to what's coming up. You're not just listening to the words that are being said, you're listening with your heart. I would say it transformed me."

Theresa, prison warden

"The inmates are now looking at each other as individuals, they're able to meet themselves and understand that we all are human, we all have issues, and that's made for a lot safer environment both for our inmates and our staff. They're learning to listen without judgment, they're learning empathy, and that's huge."

Tony, nonprofit organization leader

"We start every staff meeting, every Monday, with the council practice. Because it creates a container, we are going to be in this together now, and we're going to make it our sacred time together. And we intentionally set aside every Monday morning no matter how busy we are."

PART 2

DEEPENING THE PRACTICE OF COUNCIL: SEASONS OF AWARENESS

This section of the book is intended to focus on and support the development of four different aspects of mindful awareness:

Physical

> our bodies, other people, our surroundings, that which we can sense, feel, see, hear, taste, smell

Mental

> our thoughts, perspectives, ideas, biases, inner dialogue and misconceptions

Emotional

> our feelings: sadness, joy, fear, loneliness, love—and everything else that stirs in our hearts

Social and Energetic

> our relationships with others, and the spirit, essence, and mysteries of life

By breaking down our experience of life into these four aspects, or seasons, we start to think about a map of how it is to be human. This map is reminiscent of many models of the human experience that have been helpful to many people over time. Some may see parallels to the work of psychologist Carl Jung and four distinct "archetypes." Others may recognize a "medicine wheel" cosmology developed by many indigenous traditions to help understand the path of life. Or one might think of the seasons that make up a year. Breaking things down into these four ways of looking at how we experience the world is one of many ways of understanding being human.

We may find it useful to work with this map of the four aspects of awareness as we chart a course of inner exploration. This journey will ask us to deepen our practice of "listening from the heart," one of the most important components, or intentions, of council. In this case, the listening extends beyond the sounds we hear with our ears to paying attention to the many ways we interact with our inner life and perceive the world around us.

As we become more conscious of the way we show up in our lives, we develop greater capacity to perceive and understand ourselves and the world around us on the level of the body and our senses ("physical"), the mind and our constant thought-stream ("mental"), the heart and our range of feelings ("emotional"), and the relationships we have with the world around us, the gut sense we have about situations in which we find ourselves and the way we encounter the mysteries of life ("social and energetic"). Exploring these four categories can help us understand and become more skillful in navigating our way through the world. As we choose to pay more attention to listening deeply to ourselves and the world around us, we can build our capacity to work with these aspects of awareness through regular mindfulness activities and opportunities for reflection that we do independently, as well as what we experience when we come together in council.

What follows is a succession of twenty-four assignments—six assignments for each of the seasons of awareness. If you take on one assignment per week, you will progress through these in about six months. The assignments can also be spread out—or can be done more quickly. There is no correct way to take this on—each assignment will reveal itself to have many layers. You may well find yourself taking some extra time to ponder aspects that resonate. You may even be drawn to return to these ideas and questions again and again. We recommend that you not rush through this process. You can always come back and do things again. In fact, you may find that some of these assignments may become part of a routine you take on to practice being more mindful throughout your day and over time.

The path through these assignments is not intended to lead to a finish line where all problems are solved, mysteries are revealed and great success is guaranteed. Rather, you may consider this a journey around a great wheel of life that we never stop moving along, returning again and again to these considerations as we move through the days and years, spiraling a little deeper each time around.

Each of the twenty-four assignments that follow will be labeled with a subtheme, relating to the four categories of awareness. The first six assignments will be related to the *physical*. The next six will be related to the *mental*. Then, six related to the *emotional*. Finally, six related to the *social and energetic*. The six subthemes for each category will point to a separate element of that aspect of awareness.

In each of the assignments, you will be introduced to a new "Awareness Practice" that you can complete *as many times as you like*. These practices are offered to help you learn more about a particular aspect of yourself. Each practice is something that cannot be done wrong—it is intended to be a way for you to actively investigate the theme in a new way. You may try the practice once, or you may repeat it many times. You may find that you want to jump into the practice immediately, or you may plan for it, set a time to do it, and then spend some time reflecting or writing about your experience. Each activity is deceptively simple—it can be done in a rushed and superficial way, or in a way that really makes you think and reflect and maybe become aware of something you'd never really considered. We hope you will choose the latter approach! The experiences of these activities are for you to create and discover in your own way.

A note on the 24 Awareness Practices: Zen Teacher (and pediatrician) Jan Chozen Bays, MD, has written a great deal about simple practices for honing awareness that you can do anywhere. She was kind enough to offer permission for us to include many of these in our curriculum. Her additional writing on this topic is highly recommended, including her set of "Mindfulness On the Go" Cards, from which many of these activities are adapted.

Every assignment will also contain "Something to Consider." As the theme unfolds for you and you take some time to work with the Awareness Practice, Something to Consider will point you toward ways in which the theme may be showing up in your awareness and may lead you to some contemplation, reflection or, perhaps, to writing or journaling on this theme. Maybe this will simply sit as a question for the week, or a topic to notice in the conversations, random thoughts and discoveries that unfold. There is much to unpack around these themes and you may find new elements that are relevant to you as you come back to these suggestions for consideration. Notice what captures your attention and give yourself some space to explore these considerations.

The "Prompts" for each of the 24 subthemes are a way for you to engage, reflect and practice more deeply. The journaling you may do around these prompts is for your own benefit, self-growth, and ongoing insight; this is not an assignment you will be graded on. You can keep this writing private or share it with others, that is up to you. If you are part of a group that is meeting in council, you might suggest to the council facilitator ways to integrate the prompts offered in your weekly assignments—but please be mindful of the way your council group functions and respect the protocols established by the group.

Should you have the opportunity, you are encouraged to engage in your own councils, independently, and you may want to use these prompts and themes in councils you create and facilitate outside of an official group. Councils may be held informally, perhaps with friends or family, or you may create space for your own "solo council," if you prefer. This might be considered "a council of one" and you may feel inspired to imagine the presence of several others, listening for how they might respond to the prompts and allowing yourself to speak or write what comes up for you.

If you decide to engage in a solo council, you may find the section that follows of interest. Here we lay out the elements of council and how the steps we take might look in a group setting, as well as when we practice in a "council of one."

1. Create a circle

WHEN WE SIT IN COUNCIL
TOGETHER

Place chairs in a circle, enough for everyone, making sure everyone can see everyone else. Consider leaving one chair empty for those who are not here.

WHEN WE SIT IN COUNCIL
AS AN INDIVIDUAL

Prepare a calm space, without distraction, set out a pen or pencil and a fresh piece of paper to use. Have the prompt for today available to review. Imagine a contained space into which you will step into council.

2. Set the center

TOGETHER

Place a centerpiece cloth, add meaningful personal talking pieces, place something to ring or notate dedications, make it special.

AS AN INDIVIDUAL

Imagine things arranged in a circle with a distinct center. Find one or more items that hold meaning for you and place in front of you.

3. Arrive and bring your full attention to the circle

TOGETHER

Focus on your body, place your feet squarely on the floor, feel the chair beneath you, pay attention to your breath, gather your attention on here and now.

AS AN INDIVIDUAL

Prepare the same as noted in the left hand column: take a few deep breaths, calm your mind, separate yourself from the distractions around you, relax into the moment.

4. Offer dedications

WHEN WE SIT IN COUNCIL
TOGETHER

Facilitator invites dedications from the participants.

WHEN WE SIT IN COUNCIL
AS AN INDIVIDUAL

Think about what you want to "call into the circle"— a person, an idea, a place, speak a name or thought out loud or to yourself or write it down.

5. Check-in round

TOGETHER

Speed round noting how this moment feels: physically, mentally, emotionally, spiritually.

AS AN INDIVIDUAL

Find a word or two to describe how it is right now in your body, mind, heart, soul. Note that to yourself or write it down.

6. Prompt

TOGETHER

Facilitator offers a prompt and participants respond to that (or anything else).

AS AN INDIVIDUAL

Read the prompt provided in the assignment in this book—or use a prompt that you have come up with on your own.

Listen from the heart

TOGETHER

Set aside judgment, analyzing, agree-ing/disagreeing... and listen like you listen to music or nature.

AS AN INDIVIDUAL

Don't second guess yourself. Trust what is stirred up by the prompt and your reaction.

Speak from the heart

WHEN WE SIT IN COUNCIL **TOGETHER**	WHEN WE SIT IN COUNCIL **AS AN INDIVIDUAL**
When you receive the talking piece, say what is alive and true for you in the moment.	Write without editing or self-censoring, go with what comes up for you. Don't worry about perfect spelling or grammar. Draw an image if you don't have words. Use another language if that's easier.

Be spontaneous

TOGETHER	**AS AN INDIVIDUAL**
Don't rehearse or repeat what you had planned or what you think you should say. Let what is real and true be spoken.	Trust that what is coming up is true and needs to be written out, even if you think it doesn't make sense. Don't worry about it coming out "perfectly" —nobody is grading this.

Be lean

TOGETHER	**AS AN INDIVIDUAL**
Say what is needed. Go to the essence of what needs to be said.	Focus on what feels like it needs to be expressed. This is not about being short, just staying on topic and going to the essence of what you want to say.

7. Witness round

<table>
<tr><td>WHEN WE SIT IN COUNCIL
TOGETHER</td><td>WHEN WE SIT IN COUNCIL
AS AN INDIVIDUAL</td></tr>
<tr><td>Facilitator offers a speed round in which the group can reflect on something that stuck with you.</td><td>Set your pen down and take a breath, maybe get up and stretch, then re-read your writing as if you are hearing it for the first time.</td></tr>
</table>

8. Close

TOGETHER

AS AN INDIVIDUAL

Facilitator helps the group mark the end of the session, coming together, celebrating the time, and stepping out of council together.

Fold your paper up and set it aside. Take a deep breath and breathe out – imagining your breath carrying your words to those who might read them, or hear them in a council circle. Imagine the regard and goodwill they have as they hear your truth; acknowledge the items you placed in your center, pick them up, if you can, and offer care and respect, then return them to where you keep them.

It is up to you to decide what you do with your share – keep it safe, send it to a loved one who will be receptive to it, or tear it up if you prefer. The writing is an opportunity for you to explore what is alive in you more than anything else. Moving out of the council space gives you some distance from the "you" that responded to that prompt. Step away from this time with respect and appreciation for your inner voice and the opportunity to reflect.

You will find that council can be experienced in many ways, even after the circle has ended. Embodying council is a much deeper practice than participating in a council group once a week. Council is a way of walking in the world, intentional and present to the moment, open to all, available to experience the world around you, fresh and new in every moment.

Finally, each assignment will end with some "Resources," which are summarized for this book in short passages, but are available at greater length through the internet links provided. These links will not be relevant for those who do not have internet access; many are recordings, videos or articles that are available online and may be discovered when the time is right. Unfortunately, the limitations of space do not allow for a complete transcript of the material, so what is included within each assignment will provide a taste and will hopefully whet your appetite to do further research on the ideas and themes that interest you.

What follows are the twenty-four assignments, six corresponding to each of the seasons of awareness. May these be helpful as you continue to deepen your journey of self-awareness and insight, listening from the heart to all that arises. The opportunities to learn and deepen are ever-present.

Physical Awareness

We begin with *physical awareness*: what do we learn as we observe our bodies, the world around us, the objects, shapes, people, surroundings, etc.? How do we sense, perceive and interact with the physical world?

Physical Awareness

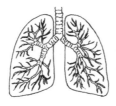

Body Language

PHYSICAL

Awareness Practice
Be Mindful of Your Posture

Several times a day, become aware of your posture. One good time to work with mindfulness of posture is when you are eating. Other interesting times include while standing in line, lying down in bed, and while walking.

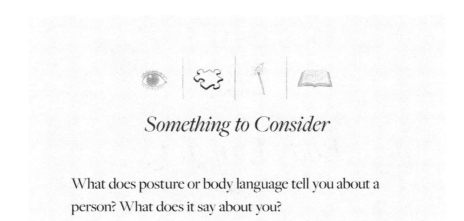

Something to Consider

What does posture or body language tell you about a person? What does it say about you?

Prompts

1) Tell a story about a time you felt physically powerful—or when you felt weak.

2) Describe a time that you listened to your body, or a time that you ignored it.

Resources

Our posture and body language impacts our views about ourselves more than we might think. In her TED Talk, Amy Cuddy talks about how we are constantly making judgements about other people's body language, but sometimes forget that we are also being impacted by the ways we are posing and expressing ourselves through body language. For example, we open up when we feel powerful. We physically spread out, open up our arms and lift our heads up when we feel proud and strong. We also close up and make ourselves physically smaller when we feel sad, weak, and powerless. Cuddy wanted to find out whether our body language influences how we think and feel about ourselves. To answer this, she conducted a small experiment where she asked a group of people to do high-power poses; like standing with your hands on your hips (like Wonder Woman) or sitting in a chair with your hands behind your head and your feet up on a table. By having them change to these postures for two minutes, Cuddy found that people felt more powerful and had lower stress levels afterwards than before they did these poses. She concluded that posture can significantly increase your confidence and make you feel more calm when you're in situations that can be stressful, like job interviews, talking in a big group, or other social settings.

Watch the TEDTalk: *Your Body Language May Shape Who You Are*
(https://c4c.link/01A)

Some people seem to rebound from stressful situations better than others. One neuroscience researcher, Peter Strick, was curious about people's stress response and what modulates it. He had noticed how elite athletes had an ability to make mistakes, but very quickly recover and continue competing. Strick's kids had told him he ought to work out his core—for example with yoga or Pilates—but, being a scientist, he was skeptical and said he found no scientific evidence of any nerve connections that might explain why working out your core had an impact on your ability to manage stress. The traditional view has been that our response to stress happens in a top-down manner: a place in your brain called the amygdala detects a threat, then sends the alarm through your nerves on a one-way path to the adrenal glands to make more adrenalin.

But research into how the rabies virus works made Strick take notice. Scientists had found in animal models that the nerve connections between the adrenal gland and the nervous system were vastly more complex than the previously assumed one-way message from the amygdala. Among these were connections from the muscles that control posture (our core) to the motor and sensory cortex (the parts of the brain that sense and tell us to move). And, what was most surprising to Strick, was that these connections were a *two-way street*. Meaning, not only is the brain telling the adrenal gland to make adrenalin and the core muscles to move, but the reverse is happening as well: the brain is listening to signals from these muscles, and then modulating the stress response by increasing or decreasing the release of adrenalin. With this evidence, Strick admitted his kids had been right, and had the scientific proof to show that core strengthening practices like yoga, tai chi, and Pilates have a down-regulating effect on our stress response.

Read the article: *Why One Neuroscientist Started Blasting His Core*
(https://c4c.link/01B)

Stress

PHYSICAL

Awareness Practice
Just Three Breaths

As many times a day as you are able, give the mind a short rest. For the duration of three breaths ask the inner voices to be silent. It's like turning off the inner radio or TV for a few minutes. Then, after the breaths, open all of your senses and just be aware of everything around you—colors, sounds, touch, smells.

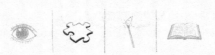

Something to Consider

What sensations are apparent in your body when you are stressed vs. when you are relaxed?

Prompts

1) Describe a time you were stressed out; what situations or people stress you out?

2) Where do you experience stress in your body and what, if anything, do you do to relieve that stress?

Resources

Are you stressed out? Do you experience difficulty sleeping, poor concentration, indigestion, heart palpitations? Although stress, in and of itself, is not a bad thing—we need it to be able to quickly respond to threat—when it is constant we experience these symptoms. Over time, even the size, structure, and function of our brains change!

Our "stress response" is largely controlled by a system called the HPA Axis. In the brain are the *hypothalamus* and the *pituitary*, and above our kidneys lie the *adrenal* glands. Communication between these when we feel under attack leads to a spike of the hormone cortisol. Cortisol has many functions: on our heart's ability to speed up and slow down, on our immune system, even at the cellular level turning genes on and off. There are also receptors for cortisol back in the hypothalamus and the pituitary, and if over time the levels of cortisol remain high, these receptors turn off and ultimately go away. It's like having a very annoying little brother who constantly calls your name—or repeatedly asks "why?" Eventually you tune him out and stop listening.

But when we're talking about "not listening" to cortisol, this means a loss of those signals that make our immune systems healthy. And in the brain, it means loss of connections between neurons, and even loss of brain mass, particularly in the frontal lobe. This is the part of the brain that helps us make decisions, have good judgement, and positive social connections. Researchers think that diseases like Alzheimer's are more likely to develop in brains that have lost their normal response to cortisol. Even more startling is research that shows that nurturing that happens in infancy (in rats, anyways), leads to normal stress response by turning on or off certain genes. Even if your rat-mother is neglectful, if you are given a nurturing rat-mother substitute, the change causes these genes to function like the rats nurtured from the start.

The thing that surprised researchers most, however, was that rats whose genes operate normally—due to nurturing in infancy—passed these normal genes on to their offspring (and conversely, those without nurturing passed on malfunctioning genes). This phenomenon is referred to as "epigenetics," and what it basically means is that we aren't simply stuck with the genes we're born with. The environment we live in plays a critical role in how our genes work in ways that aren't transient. And changes we make in our brain function can be passed on to our descendants. So, take a deep breath. In fact, take five deep, slow breaths. You just might help your HPA Axis recover its normal function and not only live a healthier life yourself, but pass this on to your future offspring!

Watch the TEDTalk: *How Stress Affects Your Brain*
(https://c4c.link/02A)

Stress (that pounding heart, sweaty palms, dry mouth) may only be bad for you if you believe it to be so! Kelly McGonigal, a psychology researcher, confesses that previously teaching people that "stress will kill you" has done damage. She cites a study of 30,000 adults, asked two questions: (1) How much stress have you experienced in the last year, and (2) Do you believe stress is bad for your health? They then looked at mortality statistics of this group. Those with a lot of stress who believed it to be harmful, had a 43% increased chance of dying. Conversely, the group with the lowest risk of dying were those with the most amount of stress but who did NOT believe stress to be harmful to their health.

So, in knowing this, McGonigal asked whether changing your view of stress can result in actual changes in your body. She explored this in another study, in which groups of people were put into a stress-provoking scenario (public speaking, a math test, and negative feedback from researchers). The first group was not given any further instructions, but the experimental group were taught that their physical responses to stress (that fast heart rate and deep breathing) were there for a reason: to prepare them for battle, in the best way for their bodies to respond. Psychologically, the second group fared much better, but what was most surprising were actual physical changes. Under the duress of stress, our hearts beat fast and our blood vessels constrict (the physiology most associated with risk of a heart attack or stroke). But in the experimental group, although their heart rates remained as high, their blood vessels actually *dilated*!

Biologically speaking, this situation is what is seen when someone experiences great joy, or awe, or courage. One aspect of our stress response is to release a hormone in the brain called oxytocin. It dilates blood vessels, dampens the immune cascade, and helps the heart repair when it's been damaged. Furthermore, oxytocin increases when we connect with others at times of duress. In another study, people were asked: (1) How much stress did you experience in the past year? And (2) How much time did you spend helping others? They found a 30% increase in risk of death for *each* major life stressor, but this risk went to zero in those who reported a high degree of caring for others. So...learn to believe that your body is perfectly made to respond to the stresses life throws at you. And the next time you're feeling overwhelmed, reach out to a friend!

Watch the TEDTalk: *How Stress Affects Your Brain*
(https://c4c.link/02B)

Sleep

PHYSICAL

Awareness Practice
Rest Your Hands

Several times a day let your hands relax completely. For at least a few seconds, let them be completely still. One way to do this is to place them in your lap and then focus your awareness on the subtle sensations you feel in the quiet hands.

Something to Consider

What's hard to let go of?

Prompts

1) What was bedtime like as a child—and how is falling asleep different now?

2) How do you feel when you've had enough sleep—or when you haven't?

Resources

Jeff Illiff is a neuroscientist who spends his time researching how brains work, especially what brains do while we are sleeping. We spend one third of our lives asleep, but what do our bodies do during this big chunk of time? Consider this: with a full night's sleep, you probably find it easier to think clearly. But nights where you hardly sleep at all, your mind probably feels foggy all day. It turns out that sleep is in part a design solution to one of our most basic problems: getting rid of waste. Most other organs in our body have special cells made for clearing out unwanted stuff, but the brain doesn't have any room for extra cells.

Before Illiff's team did their research, people didn't really know the way that the brain gets rid of waste. His team found out that the brain clears out waste in a super unique way, unlike any other part of the body. Instead of extra cells, the outsides of the blood vessels in the brain take on the role of cleaning out waste. Basically, the brain has super specialized plumbing. But this process can only happen when we're sleeping. It's kind of like the way we prioritize work: during the week, we're so busy working that we don't have much time to clean. On the weekends, we realize how dirty our living spaces got during the week and we finally have some time to clean. When the brain is in sleep mode, it finally has time to focus on clearing away that waste that builds up in between brain cells.

One waste product that Illiff's team studied is a protein called amyloid-beta. Amyloid-beta is made continually during the day, so once your brain is in sleep mode it's got plenty to do to clear it out. Researchers have noticed an association of increased amounts of amyloid-beta and Alzheimer's disease, and while it's not as though lack of sleep means you're automatically going to get Alzheimer's disease, there is some evidence that not giving enough time to clean out your brain by sleeping could contribute to the development of this disease. That's just one more reason to get a good night's sleep!

Watch the TEDTalk: *How the brain takes care of itself*
(https://c4c.link/03A)

Sleep specialist Dr. Rubin Naiman breaks down 10 common misconceptions about sleep:

1. Everyone should sleep at least eight hours every night.
Actually, how much sleep a person needs varies person by person. Someone might need 10 hours a night while someone else might need seven.

2. It's bad not to sleep the whole night through.
In reality, occasional awakenings in the middle of the night are normal.

3. You can make yourself fall asleep.
The truth is that we actually cannot control the process of falling asleep.

4. If you can't sleep, you should stay in bed and keep trying.
It's actually best to get out of bed during these times.

5. There's no way you'll have a good day if you have a bad night's sleep.
That's not necessarily true: humans are very resilient and can adapt to all kinds of conditions, including a night of little or poor sleep.

6. If you don't fall asleep right away, you aren't a good sleeper.
It's normal to take up to 20 minutes to fall asleep.

7. A lot of dreaming equates with a bad night of sleep.
That's false—dreaming every night is a key part of a good night's sleep!

8. If you can't sleep, better to be productive and get work done.
Being productive at night can actually disrupt your sleep.

9. It's normal to sleep poorly more and more as you age.
This isn't bound to happen as you age. While it's common, it is not always healthy or normal.

10. It's good to keep a watch on the clock when you can't sleep.
Watching the clock makes it harder to go back to sleep!

Read the list: *10 Mistaken Beliefs About Sleep*
(https://c4c.link/03B)

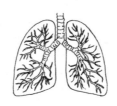

Breathing

PHYSICAL

Awareness Practice
Slowing Down

Become aware of the movement of air, both in obvious forms, such as wind or the ventilation in a room, and in subtler forms, such as the breath.

Something to Consider

How does air move around and in you?

Prompts

1) Describe a smell you love—and one you hate.

2) Tell about a time you lost your breath, or a time when you caught your breath...

Resources

Deep breathing can help dampen anxiety, bring you into the present moment, and help you slow down and consider how to respond to what is causing you stress. When you are stressed out or worried, you can physically feel it in your body, for instance through your heart beating fast or feeling dizzy.

According to Dr. Tania Elliot, who works at NYU Langone Health, the "flight or fight response" drives this reaction our body has towards stress. Because we experience constant stress in our day-to-day lives, our body is repeatedly activating this kind of response. This response arises because of minor things like work conflict, or less time to talk to friends, or because of majorly stressful situations like marriage problems or fears of losing housing. When your body starts filling with adrenalin and other stress hormones, deep breaths can help interrupt the responses that lead to dry mouth, rapid breathing and heart rate, and even the mental "hamster wheel" of thoughts.

If you want to stop feeling stressed, Ester Sternberg, a research director at the Arizona Center for Integrative Medicine, suggests that you think of it like taking your foot off of the gas and putting your foot on the brakes. To help "put your foot on the brakes," Sternberg talks about deep breathing as a way to activate your vagus nerve, which slows your heart rate and helps your body move into a state of relaxation. There are many patterns of intentional breathing that help dampen the stress response. In one, you slow your inhalation to five seconds, then exhale for five seconds. In another, Dr. Elliot suggests breathing in for four counts, then out for eight counts.

Dr. Sternberg also suggests breathing in for four counts, holding for seven, then out for eight (also known as "4-7-8 Breathing"). Try each pattern and see what works for you. Adopting a daily practice of intentionally deep breathing for one to two minutes twice a day can help control your body's overreaction to day-to-day stresses. Over time, your nervous system will be healthier!

Read the article: *What Deep Breathing Does to Your Body*
(https://c4c.link/04A)

There are always things around us that can activate our flight or fight response—loud noises, bright lights, and countless other sensory things that catch our attention. Stacey Schuerman, an experienced registered yoga teacher, says that taking a few minutes out of the day to focus on your breathing can make a real difference in your life, even though at first it seems simple or boring. In her TED Talk, Schuerman walks through one way of practicing deep breathing.

First find a comfortable position (sitting or lying) in which you are fully supported

You may close your eyes, and take a few moments to feel your feet on the ground, or the contact your back makes with the chair, or floor.

You can feel your spine lengthen as you breathe normally, and allow tight places to soften (like your jaw, or shoulder muscles).

Consciously let go of everything outside of the space you are in: things that might have happened before the practice, things you have to do after, and any judgements or expectations you have.

Notice your heartbeat and welcome yourself as you are in the moment.

Bringing awareness to your breath, notice the rise and fall of your chest as you inhale and exhale. For five breaths, count the seconds it takes for inhalation and then exhalation; commonly deep breaths last between four and eight, but whatever you count is fine...just notice.

After you are finished with your deep breaths, notice the state of your mind and body. Both may be calmer than when you began. Intentionally step away from this space and continue into your day.

Watch the TEDTalk: *Breath—Five Minutes Can Change Your Life*
(https://c4c.link/04B)

Slowing Down

PHYSICAL

Awareness Practice
Waiting

Anytime you find yourself waiting—maybe when you're in line for something—take this as an opportunity to be curious. How does your body feel? Are you impatient to move?

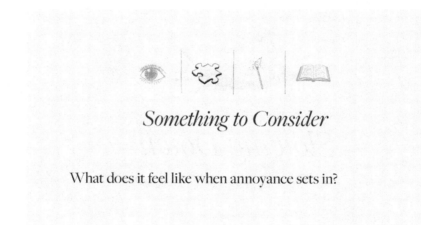

Something to Consider

What does it feel like when annoyance sets in?

Prompts

1) Talk about something in life that went too fast—or too slow.

2) What do you slow down for?

Resources

The world has been "stuck in fast forward" for a long time. In his TED Talk, Carl Honoré talks about ways in which we can all slow down to live healthier lives. We often try to make things better by speeding them up, but then lose connection to the parts of our lives where we should be slowing down. If we break free from the mindset of always moving forward quickly, and slow down at the right moments, we are actually able to accomplish more! Honoré gives many examples of ways in which slowing down is beneficial. One example is the slow food movement, in which we get more pleasure and health from the food we eat if we cook it and eat it at a steady pace. Getting food from places like farmers markets and choosing organic food can help us appreciate it more. If we take the time to slow down in other settings such as the workplace, at home and in our private spaces, quality of life improves and productivity goes up.

Honoré emphasizes the importance of taking little moments to sit alone in a quiet room without any distractions, which can help people recharge and think creatively. Taking time away from distractions to be with family and friends also creates more meaningful relationships. Although going slow might not always be the right answer, Honoré believes that there is such a thing as "good slow," where we are present with those that we care about, taking time to slow down and enjoy life. Slowing down at the right moments can help us feel like we are actually living our lives, and rather than speed through our daily routines checking off boxes, we instead cherish our lives all the more.

Watch the TEDTalk: *In Praise of Slowness*
(https://c4c.link/05A)

The world will never stop moving. Because it will always be noisy, we have to intentionally pause. Silence can help settle and calm our minds and bodies. In her podcast, Cara Bradley talks about ways in which we can take breaks from noise, to help us refresh and re-energize ourselves, resulting in a more balanced nervous system. Bradley first talks about two important things to consider when taking a pause: Outer and Inner noise. Outer noise is all of the stuff that we constantly hear around us: people talking, machines humming, iPhone alerts. Inner noise is the stuff that goes on inside of us. Bradley describes it as being in a quiet room but feeling like you are around a whole crowd of people all trying to talk to you at once. To help cut through outer and inner noise, we have to find our own outer and inner silence. To stop outer noise, Bradley talks about taking small actions, from turning off the things around us that make noise, or finding a quiet space where we can be alone. To find inner silence, taking time to pause for one to two minutes before moving on to a new task can help calm our minds and better prepare us for what we have to accomplish in the day.

Bradley also introduces the "power pause practice," in which you place your feet on the floor, hands on your thighs and close your eyes. You then turn your focus on different parts of your body, like how your feet feel on the ground, how fast or slow your heart is beating, the feel of your breath. The simple act of noticing when doing this practice can help take away some noise, making space to clear our bodies and minds.

Read the article: *The Power of Pause*

(https://c4c.link/05B)

Nutrition

PHYSICAL

Awareness Practice
When Eating, Just Eat

Choose one meal a day just to eat and not do anything else. Sit down and take the time to notice the color, shape, texture, smell and taste of your food. Attend to the smells and flavors in your mouth. Listen to the sounds of eating and drinking. Notice what is familiar and what is different.

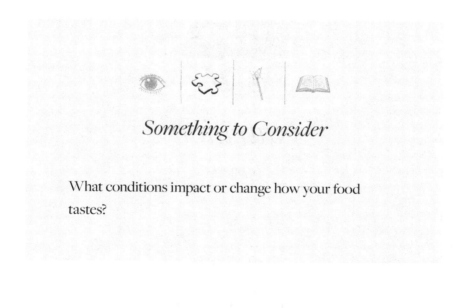

Something to Consider

What conditions impact or change how your food tastes?

Prompts

1) Growing up, what was your favorite food? Tell a story about a favorite meal.

2) What is a food that you're curious about, or that you crave?

Resources

The food you eat affects your brain! Suck all the water out of your brain and you're left with lipids (fats), protein (made up of amino acids), micronutrients, and glucose. And not all forms of each of these are created equal! As far as lipids go, your brain needs fat (which you must get in your diet) in order to make cell membranes, hormones, and transmitters. Omega 3 and 6 fatty acids are particularly important, as is the ratio between them. Ideally, a diet with a 4:1 ratio of omega 6s to omega 3s is optimal, but in our present day world of monoculture (think corn) and mega farming, this ratio has skewed to over 16:1. This translates to brain diseases like Alzheimer's. But eating foods like fatty fish (sardines, salmon, and cod) as well as nuts and seeds improves this ratio.

Proteins in our diet get broken down into amino acids, which are then used in the brain to make neurotransmitters. That post-meal slump may be the result of increased tryptophan, which when it reaches the brain gets turned into serotonin and has a sedating effect. Conversely, your late-night munching and caffeinated drinks cause increases in other neurotransmitters (like norepinephrine and dopamine) that are activating and might be the cause of your sleep disturbances. To make these neurotransmitters, your brain also needs a collection of small amounts of vitamins and micronutrients. In particular, the B vitamins (thiamine, folate, cobalamin, riboflavin), and minerals Iron, Copper, Magnesium, and Zinc are all important. In an ideal world with healthy soil, these would be present in sufficient amounts. However, again because of our farming practices, our soils may lack adequate amounts of precursors, so taking a multivitamin may be a good idea depending on where you live and your diet.

Finally, the fuel our brains rely on is glucose. Though our bodies are really good at assuring our brains have a steady supply, what you eat in a given meal can have a big impact! Foods with a high glycemic index (white sugar, processed foods, white bread, sweetened sodas) cause a quick spike in blood glucose that then rapidly drops. This can cause the post-meal jitters followed by a slump in energy. To remedy this, eat complex carbohydrates like minimally processed food, whole grains, and increased fiber. A balanced and varied diet is key to brain health.

Watch the TEDTalk: *How the Food You Eat Affects Your Brain*
(https://c4c.link/06A)

Thich Nhat Hanh, a renowned and beloved Vietnamese Buddhist monk, teacher, and author, has spent his life promoting nonviolent solutions to conflict and raising awareness of the interconnectedness of all elements in nature. He has written over 130 books and countless meditations to help us bring awareness, peace, and joy to the simple activities we may take for granted, like drinking a glass of water, washing our hands, or taking out the garbage. Here are shortened versions of four simple meditations he has shared around the way we eat and drink:

1. Seeing water: Knowing that your body itself is 70% water, and that all life on earth is sustained by water, when you turn on a water faucet can you see clear back to the source of your water? In gratitude for water we see the interrelatedness of all forms of life on our planet.

2. The bowl is empty: Of course, we are all grateful when we have a full meal. But take a moment to see the emptiness of your bowl before filling it. Know that around the world there are those for whom a full bowl of food is rare. Consider how you might help feed others.

3. The origins of a meal: Living in developed countries, we are often the recipients of food from all over the world. Consider as you begin to eat how many hands have worked, how many lives been given, how much energy was expended for this food to arrive on your plate. Take it in with the intent to put such vast effort to good use.

4. Recycling: We might prefer the smell of a rose to the smell of garbage, but can you see how they are one and the same? Nothing on this planet grows without a connection to something that has died to nourish it. Garbage becomes compost,

compost becomes rich soil, soil nourishes plants that bloom and provide food, then wilt and fade and turn again into garbage.

Read the article: *Meditations for Mindful Living*
(https://c4c.link/06B)

Mental Awareness

We now turn to *mental awareness*: what do we notice as we observe the voice in our heads, our biases and perspectives on things, the ways we think about the world, and those in it? What are the stories that we have learned to believe about ourselves, our world and our place in it?

Mental Awareness

Inner Critic, Negative Thoughts

MENTAL

Awareness Practice
Annoyance

Become aware of annoyance, when it sets in. What voice arises in your mind? Does it speak kindly, or does it criticize you, others and/or the situation? Notice when anxiety first makes its appearance in the day. Several times a day, pause and assess whether annoyance is present within you, and listen to your inner dialogue

Something to Consider

Is what your inner voice says true? Does it speak words you might say to someone you hold dear (like a grand-parent or loved one)?

Prompts

1) Tell about the first thing you can remember being blamed for.

2) Where in your life are you a hero, where are you a villain?

Resources

In his podcast *The Science of Happiness*, host Dacher Keltner talks to Steven Czifra, who has spent the last two decades in and out of prison, and who is now a graduate student at UC Berkeley. They talk about and reflect on a happiness practice called the "self-compassionate letter." In this practice, people write a letter to themselves as if they were someone else, like a mentor or a friend, and give some advice and support for situations they have gone or are going through in life. This helps people reflect on their actions and experiences from a different perspective.

In his own letter, Czifra writes that "people are not defined by their feelings or actions" and that "you should know that you are as deserving of feeling okay as anyone." He is giving himself a break for the things that have happened in his life, like the instability of his childhood, lack of care and security. Czifra reflects on his letter by saying that he developed an understanding that everyone is human and experiences both good and bad things.

In the second part of this podcast, Keltner talks to Serena Chen, a professor at UC Berkeley who studies self-compassion. Chen describes self-compassion as "being kind and understanding to yourself like you would your friends." It also includes recognizing that we are all human and will make mistakes. Chen and her team set up a study where a group of people were given an extremely hard test, designed so that everyone failed. Afterwards, half were told that "the test was a very hard test and that a lot of people also failed" (a compassion-evoking phrase). The other half were told that "even though they failed, they must be really smart to be at UC Berkeley" (a self-esteem promoting phrase). After this, the whole group had the opportunity to take the test again.

Chen and her team found that the group given the compassionate encouragement studied longer for the second test than the group given an ego-boost. She concluded that when people receive compassion, they are more motivated to do better next time. Keltner also says that other studies have shown that people who respond with compassion to their own flaws and setbacks—rather than beating themselves up about them—experience greater physical and mental health, and seem to bounce back more easily from stress and challenges.

Read the article: *Quieting Your Inner Critic*
(https://c4c.link/07A)

A negative outlook can impact our lives in more ways than we think. A negative outlook can increase the risk of poor health (mental and physical), and problems with relationships and finances. As a cognitive behavioral therapist, Amy Morin has seen the ways that changing thought patterns can impact your life. She describes some practices that help people change their outlook on life. The practice that she focuses on in this article was created by PracticeWise and teaches people how to turn *blue* thoughts into true thoughts.

The acronym B.L.U.E. stands for:

Blaming myself: Self-blame can lead to depression and other mental health problems.

Looking for Bad News: Focusing on the bad parts of the day keeps you "stuck in a dark place."

Unhappy guessing: We predict doom and gloom, even though we don't know what tomorrow will bring.

Exaggeratedly negative: The habit of expanding negativity to all aspects of a situation.

Morin has some suggestions for turning these *blue* thoughts into true thoughts. First, she suggests asking yourself, "what would I say to a friend who had this problem?" She also suggests thinking about a realistic, positive action that you can take in the moment to change a negative thought. This can help you shape what you want your future to look like. Morin writes that "studies show changing your thoughts physically alters your brain over time." If you intentionally think positively, then you will start to see yourself and your abilities with less negativity and more hope.

Read the article: *The Beginner's Guide to Recognizing and Changing Negative Thoughts*
(https://c4c.link/07B)

Perspective and View

MENTAL

Awareness Practice
Entering New Spaces

A shorthand for this practice is "mindfulness of doors," but it actually involves bringing awareness to any transitions between spaces, when you leave one kind of space and enter another. Before you walk through a door, pause, even if only for a second, and take one breath. Notice when you or others barge into a space. Be aware of the differences you might feel in each new space you enter.

Something to Consider

What are the doorways you enjoy passing through and what are those you don't?

Prompts

1) Describe an event in your life that caused everything to change.

2) When you pass through the next major transition in your life, what will be different?

Resources

Dan Harris, former ABC anchorman, now meditation promoter, touts the wide-ranging benefits of meditation. From lowering blood pressure, to decreasing symptoms of irritable bowels or psoriasis, to augmenting a healthy immune response, meditation is more and more being proven in studies to be beneficial. A Harvard study showed that short, daily "doses" of meditation actually *grew* grey matter in the brain in areas noted to be active in empathy and compassion, and caused grey matter to *shrink* in areas associated with the stress response. At Yale, researchers have looked at what parts of the brain are active when we are "doing nothing" (a misnomer, because our brains are never really doing nothing).

The active nerves are collectively called the Default Mode Network (DMN), and in long-time meditators, their DMN's turn out to be quieter not only during meditation sessions, but even when they are not actively meditating. They conclude that this dampening of the "chatter" of memory and worry that we usually flick back and forth between is what allows us to "be in the zone," as is often talked about amongst athletes when they are completely present and undistracted. Indeed, it is why Marines, elite athletes, corporate business people, lawyers, and doctors are turning to meditation in order to be better at what they do. Harris predicts that meditation is the next health revolution. Citing how running was viewed in the 1940s (if you went for a run, people would ask "from what?"), and how today it is universally accepted that exercise is a must, and people who don't do it feel guilty, Harris postulates that before long the health-conscious thing one must do is meditate.

Watch the video: *Hack Your Brain's Default Mode with Meditation*
(https://c4c.link/08A)

Mindfulness offers a chance to be with discomfort—achy knees, a busy mind, pesky emotions. Rather than run away, or distract ourselves, or self-soothe with food or alcohol; we learn that we can tolerate being uncomfortable and grant ourselves permission to be exactly as we are...no changes necessary. The following is a practice described by Dr. Mark Bertin. Bertin suggests you listen to the audio (linked below), but if you can't do that, he says it's okay to read through this text and then go back and read a few sentences, work through the practice, and continue to the end. He suggests you do this seated and that you allot about 15-minutes:

Sit for a few minutes, bringing attention to the sensation of breathing. Your mind will stay busy; just notice that thoughts are thoughts, and then patiently redirect attention to the breath. Now bring to mind something minor that you don't like that much about yourself. Choose something uncomfortable, but not overwhelming. Notice what arises. It might be a sense of physical discomfort, or an emotion, or an anxious thought. Give attention to all of it: the facts, your reactions, emotions like disappointment or frustration, and anything else that comes up. If the practice becomes too uncomfortable, take care of yourself. Allow yourself a break, seek out support, and let go of the practice for now. Come back to whatever feels most appropriate in this moment. Acknowledge what you experience right now as best as you can, without any need to fix or change anything for this moment. For the next few minutes, on each in-breath, be aware that this is a challenge for you right now, and that all people have challenges. On each out-breath, wish yourself the same happiness and wellness that you'd wish for your best friend. To end, come back to the simple focus on the sensation of your breath. If your eyes have been closed, open them and look around, re-orienting to the room. No matter how long you've done this practice, give yourself credit and appreciation before you move into the rest of your day.

Read the article: *A Mindfulness Practice to Cultivate Non-Judgmental Awareness* (https://c4c.link/08B)

Bias

MENTAL

Awareness Practice
See Color

Become aware of the colors that appear in your environment. Pick a color, and look for it in unexpected places. Notice different shades.

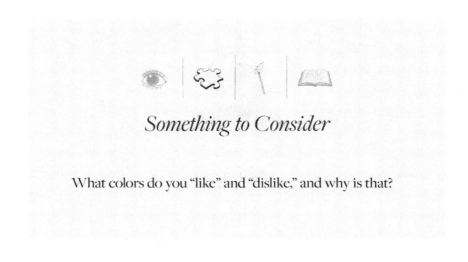

Something to Consider

What colors do you "like" and "dislike," and why is that?

Prompts

1) Tell the story of someone in your life whose behavior is so predictable.

2) What is something you've always done a certain way that doesn't really make sense to repeat?

Resources

There are many prejudices that we hold against people who don't share our race, ethnicity, gender, religion, or political beliefs. Scientists are trying to study where these prejudices come from and how we can begin to break down these barriers. The practice of mindfulness—the state of being that involves increased awareness of our emotions, thoughts, and surroundings—might be one way to reduce prejudice and bias. For example, one study found that a short mindfulness training reduced unconscious bias against Black people and elderly people. Why might this be? Scientists break it down into three possible reasons. Firstly, mindfulness can help people see the full picture. Not only do humans have a natural tendency to quickly judge people for their differences, but we also are swift to blame others for what we perceive as their mistakes.

We often fail to see the outside factors that can lead to bad outcomes. An example of this is the reaction of many white Americans to the people of color who did not leave New Orleans during Hurricane Katrina: they assumed that the people were too stubborn to leave rather than recognizing that they lacked money or the means to evacuate. Recent studies show that mindfulness can help us see one another as products of our circumstances rather than bad people who do bad things.

Secondly, mindfulness helps us give equal attention to the positive things in life rather than focus on the negative things. As humans, the "negativity bias" has proven to have survival benefits: if you are programmed to see threats quickly you're more likely to pass down your genes. But in today's world, having a strong negativity bias can lead us to constantly assume that the worst will happen. Negativity bias is particularly high in social situations where we interact with groups that are different than our own, partly because we fear rejection. Evidence suggests that mindfulness can help decrease the impact of negativity bias and therefore help us be more open to social interactions outside our group.

A third benefit of mindfulness in dismantling racial bias is that mindfulness may be able to help us take the position of others (empathy) and see them as equal to ourselves. It is human nature to try to maintain a positive image of ourselves in our mind. Though in itself this is not a bad trait, it can also make us more likely to put others down in order to feel better about ourselves. For example, if your boss tells your whole group to improve on something, it is common to assume that your boss is directing that feedback at everyone else in the group except for you. This tendency is called the self-positivity bias. Some recent research has shown that people who actually practiced mindfulness demonstrated less self-positivity bias than those who just learned about the benefits of mindfulness.

We already know that mindfulness does great things for our personal wellbeing. New evidence seems to suggest that mindfulness can also improve our relationships with others, especially those who are very different from us.

Read the article: *Three Ways Mindfulness Can Make You Less Biased*
(https://c4c.link/09A)

Cognitive biases are hardwired in our brains, or are learned and refined by repetition; they color how we see the world. Here is a list of twenty cognitive biases that can negatively affect our decision making.

1. *Anchoring bias*: the tendency to put a lot of stock in the first piece of information heard. For example, in a business negotiation, the first person to make a bid decides the range of amounts that will be considered reasonable for the rest of the negotiation.

2. *Availability heuristic*: overrating the importance of the information that is close at hand. A person who had a loved one who smoked three packs a day and lived to be 100 years old might be more likely to believe that smoking is not unhealthy.

3. *Bandwagon effect*: a belief becomes more popular based on how many other people hold that belief. This is a form of groupthink that occurs when people lose their sense of individuality and conform to a group.

4. *Blind-spot bias*: the tendency to easily see faults in others while ignoring their presence in ourselves.

5. *Choice-supportive bias*: simply put, we like the things we choose. In fact, we like them more just because we chose them even if our choice has significant flaws. For example, people still love their dogs even if they bite people.

6. *Clustering illusion*: people try to find patterns in complete random events. For example, gamblers often believe that a red is more or less likely to come up on a roulette table after a string of reds, when in reality the previous color has nothing to do with which comes next.

7. *Confirmation bias*: when seeking out new information, we tend to prefer the things that confirm what we already believe. This is why it's so hard to change someone else's mind even when you bring facts to an argument.

8. *Conservatism bias*: the tendency to favor our prior beliefs over new ones. This is why it took people so long to change their false belief that the earth was flat.

9. *Information bias*: people have a tendency to seek out lots of information—sometimes too much. We can actually make more accurate predictions with less information, so more information is not always better.

10. *Ostrich effect*: when we know dangerous or negative information is coming, we tend to do everything we can to ignore it. Like an ostrich, we bury our heads in the sand—out of sight, out of mind.

11. *Outcome bias*: the tendency to judge decisions based on the perceived outcome of that decision. For example, if someone went to Vegas to gamble and won a lot of money, they would think that they made a great decision. However, had the outcome been a financial loss, the decision would be deemed a bad one.

12. *Overconfidence*: overestimating one's abilities and knowledge, which can lead to taking greater risks. This bias is more common among people who consider themselves experts on a certain topic, since they tend to be more confident that they are right.

13. *Placebo effect*: when we expect something to have a certain effect on us, we tend to convince ourselves that the effect is taking place even if it isn't. For example, people given fake pills often experience the same effects as someone given a real pill.

14. *Pro-innovation* bias: proponents of a new invention like to exaggerate its usefulness and underestimate its drawbacks.

15. *Recency*: people highly favor new information over older information. For example, when investors are looking at trends in the stock market, they tend to overlook older patterns and make bad decisions.

16. *Salience*: Humans often focus on the most easily recognizable parts of a person or concept. This explains the inability to see the uniqueness of people of color if you were raised in a community that did not include them.

17. *Selective perception*: we allow our preferences and expectations to shift how we see the world. If you're watching a basketball game with your favorite team playing against your rival, you're going to see the other team's fouls more than the team you're rooting for.

18. *Stereotyping*: when we approach someone that we don't know, we make assumptions about them based on their external characteristics lacking any real information about them.

19. *Survivorship bias*: humans tend to focus on examples of people who have succeeded, which can lead us to make false judgments about a situation. For example, one might think that it is easy to succeed as an entrepreneur because we hear so many success stories about them. However, we easily forget how many stories of failure are also out there.

20. *Zero-risk bias*: people love and crave 100% certainty, even if it is not productive and holds us back. We often choose options in which we can guarantee zero risk over a more favorable option that only has a 1% chance of risk.

We're all subject to these biases, so once you learn to recognize them in yourself you can become a better decision maker.

See the full chart: *20 Cognitive Biases that Screw Up Your Decisions* (https://c4c.link/09B)

Changing Your Mind

MENTAL

Awareness Practice
Look Up!

Several times a day, deliberately look up. Take a few minutes to really look at the ceiling in rooms, or at the sky. See what new things you notice. Are there small things you have never noticed but are revealed when you concentrate?

Something to Consider

What's new in your landscape? What perspectives have shifted for you recently?

Prompts

1) Tell about a time you changed your mind—what happened?

2) What's a misconception people have about you?

Resources

Unlearning hatred starts with compassion. In his TED Talk, Christian Picciolini talks about the ways that people can head down the wrong paths. As a kid, Picciolini was always bullied and would be made fun of for his name, until one day a stranger noticed him and did not make fun of his name or his heritage—he instead welcomed him and accepted him for who he was. Picciolini says this man was America's first neo-Nazi skinhead leader. Picciolini was welcomed into the Nazi movement, where he began to believe the lies they spread about Jewish people, people of color, and immigrants. So powerful was the urge to belong, that he embraced ideologies that he later realized were not his own. In continuing down this dark path, he was violent towards people because of their skin color and made racist music that continues to influence white supremacy supporters today.

Picciolini says that being part of this hate-filled group gave him a purpose, identity and sense of community that he lacked. He reflects that people develop hate to fill a void in themselves, and realized that hate for other people started with hate for himself. Rather than feel insecure, he inflicted pain on other people. For Picciolini, things began to change when he married a girl that was not in the Nazi movement and they had their first son. He began to question his identification with the community that he was a part of. He tried to slowly step back from the movement, but still couldn't let go completely.

As the owner of a record store that sold white-power music, but also other forms of music that drew in different people, Picciolini became friends with people that he had been taught to hate. He realized that he had more in common with them than he thought, and began to change because of these people who showed him compassion when he did not deserve it. Today, he's the founder of the Free Radicals project, where he works to help people disengage from hate groups. Picciolini believes that hate is learned and love is "a natural instinct" that is suppressed by hate. Furthermore, he thinks people can be pulled out of the hatred that they learn with compassion and understanding.

Watch the TEDTalk: *How Do You Unlearn Hatred?*
(https://c4c.link/10A)

Listening to each other requires more effort than we think. For Dave Isay, a radio producer, it was hard to listen to his father when he told Dave that he was gay. They had been really close all of Isay's life and this completely shocked him. Isay's dad told him about the Stonewall riots, where Black and Latino drag queens fought back against police at a gay bar in Manhattan in 1969, sparking the gay rights movement. Isay was interested in learning more about these events and decided to track down everyone he could find who had been at the Stonewall Inn during the riots. For Isay, recording their stories and conversations gave him the chance to connect with and understand his dad's experience. He learned that gay people before Stonewall had to hide who they were out of shame and pain.

After this project, Isay continued to make more documentaries on people whose stories were previously untold and who were made to feel like they didn't matter. He found that listening can be a form of respect and can give people dignity. Having learned this for himself, Isay wanted to give more people the chance to listen to one another through a project called StoryCorps. In this project, people are put in a booth together where they can talk to each other about their own stories and share things they don't usually talk about. For Isay, these booths are a way to learn to love people because of the stories they tell. For Isay, "you can't hate someone whose story you've heard." These conversations can help us "recognize our shared humanity" and show that every life matters.

Watch the TEDTalk: *How Do We Change When We
Really Listen To The People We Love?*
(https://c4c.link/10B)

Attention/Focus

MENTAL

Awareness Practice
Are You Overlooking Something?

Several times a day, pause to notice what you're paying attention to at that moment. What is right in front of you that you don't notice at first. Open your senses to see if you can identify something you've been failing to notice. A sound? A smell? Something others are aware of that you tend to ignore?

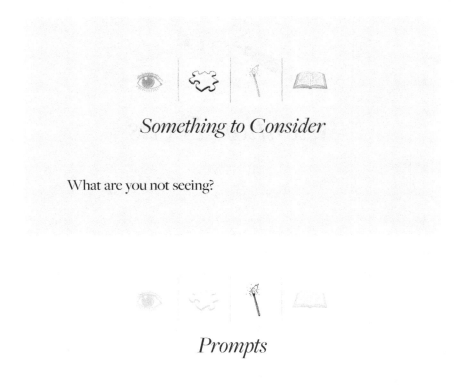

Something to Consider

What are you not seeing?

Prompts

1) What is something you do on autopilot—and what usually distracts you?

2) What helps you focus?

Resources

Attention is like a flashlight. What we shine light on in a dark room immediately becomes visible. Attention helps focus our mind on specific things around us or things inside us, but distracted thinking and stress disrupt our focus and attention. Dr. Amishi Jha, from the University of Miami, says that our minds wander for half of the time we are awake as they move constantly between things that have happened or will happen, even when we want to be paying attention. Jha points out, however, that ruminating on things that distract us is different from day-dreaming, where we are given the opportunity to think creatively and be spontaneous. Worrying about past events that we cannot change or future scenarios we cannot predict prevents us from having the mental space to think creatively. Jha emphasizes how important having daily practices are to help give our minds the space to have creative thoughts, and notes that this also helps us have more positive moods. Something as small as taking breaks can help us focus our attention on the things that matter to us.

Watch the TEDTalk: *How Can We Pay Better Attention To Our Attention?*
(https://c4c.link/11A)

In his book, *Focus*, Daniel Goleman posits that Emotional Intelligence is composed of self-awareness and empathy, and that both of these develop through strengthening our attention. He goes on to talk about three different types of focus—Inner, Other, and Outer. Attention to our Inner state is a matter of "being aware that you are aware." In order to reach a point where you can do something about your overblown temper, you've got to develop an awareness of what's going on in your inner world that causes anger to arise. With respect to Other awareness, Goleman speaks of the need to develop intention to maintain focus on a person you want to be with, rather than being distracted by every ping or blip of your phone. The third type of awareness—Outer—is more elusive. Goleman describes it as awareness of systems, both micro and macro, that we must put effort into learning because we simply don't have the sensory apparatus to directly experience things like global warming. But developing awareness and attention to these Outer phenomena is vital to our wellbeing. He goes so far as to say that developing the ability to focus in all three realms isn't just a matter of getting good at something, it's the "key to a fulfilling life." The good news is that attentional ability can be practiced and improved, and doesn't require sitting on a mountaintop or retreating to a monastery.

Goleman thinks attentional practices should be built into elementary education, and as an example talks about a school in Spanish Harlem where second graders have sessions every day where they watch and count their breath. Researchers have found that exercises like this enhance "cognitive control," which turns out to be a better predictor of success in life than IQ or socioeconomic status.

Read the article: *Is Attention the Secret to Emotional Intelligence?*
(https://c4c.link/11B)

Mind Wandering

MENTAL

Awareness Practice
Empty Space

Every once in a while, shift your awareness from objects to the space around the objects. For example, when you look in the mirror, notice the space around the image of your head. In a room, at home or outside, notice the empty space rather than the furniture, people, or other visual objects.

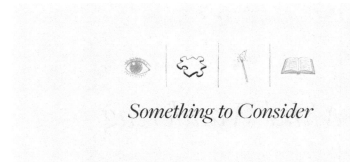

Something to Consider

How are you affected by your environment and how are others affected by theirs?

Prompts

1) Tell about a time your head was somewhere else.

2) Tell about a time you were "in the zone" and not distracted by things going on around you.

Resources

What does a wandering mind do? Though some studies support the tenet that "a healthy mind is a focused mind," others suggest that mind-wandering, or day-dreaming, is essential to creativity, improved mood and increased productivity. Probably best known is the association between mind-wandering and creativity. Participants in a recent study on this topic who were allowed time to wander during a task came up with more novel uses for day to day items. The relationship between mind-wandering and mood is less clear. Though when asked about the content of their mind's musings, people more often reported negative thoughts; if they engaged in interesting off-task musings (wandering) their mood consistently became more positive.

Researchers noted a distinction between mind-wandering and ruminating, or obsessing over negative thoughts; ruminating did not lead to improvements in performance, but subjects did better with performing mindless tasks when they were encouraged to wander. Their reaction times improved, as well as the sheer number of tasks they accomplished. Authors noted, however, that tasks that require a high degree of focus (for example, brain surgery) do not similarly benefit from mind-wandering. Finally, mind-wandering was associated with more creative goal setting, as well as the ability to forego immediate reward for the sake of realizing a more important goal in the future.

Read the article: *How Mind-Wandering May Be Good For You*
(https://c4c.link/12A)

It is the nature of our minds to wander. Just ask anyone who has decided to start a meditation practice, only to become discouraged at their lack of ability to quiet their thoughts. In a recent study, over 2000 adults were pinged throughout the day to report on what was in their mind at the moment. A whopping 47% of the time found them thinking "wandering thoughts," not associated with the task at hand!

Knowing that, evolutionarily speaking, our bodies don't tend to hang on to traits that aren't useful, researchers decided to look into what it might be about mind-wandering that *is* useful. Although the goal in focused-attention meditation is to keep one's mind on one target (the breath, or a word, etc.), both brand-new and long-time meditators will tell you that this often doesn't happen. In fact, it is that moment in which you recognize your mind has wandered and you pull it back into focus that really matters.

As researchers looked at images of brains while the participant meditated, pressing a button when they noticed their mind wandering and again when it returned to focusing, they consistently noticed about 12 seconds of quite predictable activity in specific brain regions. These areas start out to be most active in the Default Mode Network just before the first button, followed by the attentional parts of the brain at the time of button press, and finally the executive (or decision-making) portions, until the time of refocus and the second button press. The longer the participant's experience with meditation, the quieter the basal activity of the DMN and the more connectivity between the DMN and attentional and executive areas.

Researchers also remarked that training your brain is a lot like going to the gym. If you want to build a muscle, you need resistance. A bicep will bulk up the more weight it is asked to lift. Mind-wandering is a lot like using weights to train the brain: it is the resistance needed in order to develop the "muscle" of meditative focus.

Read the article: *How to Focus a Wandering Mind*
(https://c4c.link/12B)

Emotional Awareness

We now look to *emotional awareness*: how do our feelings and emotions work, what control do we have over them? How do we recognize and identify emotional states? What can we learn about what causes emotions, how they impact our thoughts and actions, and how we can shift them?

Emotional Awareness

Emotion Regulation

EMOTIONAL

Awareness Practice
Bottoms of the Feet

As often as possible during the day, direct your awareness to the bottoms of your feet. Become aware of the sensations in the bottoms of the feet, such as the pressure of the floor, your socks or shoes, the ground beneath them or their warmth or coolness. Try this when you notice yourself becoming anxious or upset.

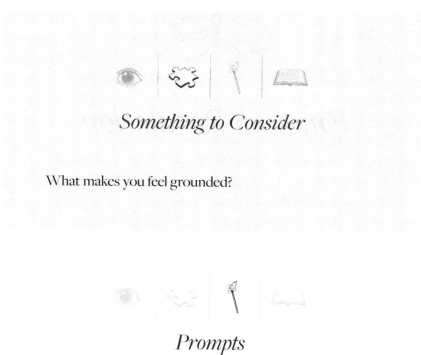

Something to Consider

What makes you feel grounded?

Prompts

1) Tell about a time you flew off the handle—describe your emotions, as you remember them, and whether there was a moment you caught yourself (or might have) in order to shift and change the outcome.

2) Talk about a time someone was upset and you responded to help them—what

did you do and how did it work out?

Resources

It's common to think that emotions are pre-existing states in our brains that emerge when something triggers them. But as Lisa Feldman Barrett explains, emotions are really just guesses and predictions that our brains make in the moment. "Emotions are not built in. They are built." When we experience something that we have not before, we ask ourselves what it is most similar to, based on our past experiences in order to predict what this new experience will be like.

Rather than assuming that all smiles mean someone is happy, Barrett suggests that we make emotions meaningful by connecting them to our own situation, which might include smiling at a sad memory, or crying because we are in fact happy. Barrett suggests that feelings like calmness, excitement, comfort, agitation, and discomfort are not our emotions. Rather, these are just responses to what is going on in our bodies. Our brain makes predictions to try and understand these feelings so that we know what to do with them. Take, for instance, the feeling of your stomach churning. If the context is that you are standing outside a bakery you like to go to because they bake the best chocolate chip cookies, your brain is going to contextualize that stomach churning as anticipation of a yummy treat. However, if you're sitting in a doctor's office awaiting test results feeling the same stomach churning, your brain will lay on the very different emotion of dread.

Barrett wishes to emphasize that "emotions that seem to happen to you are made by you." In realizing this, we are given the option of considering any number of potential causes and responses to a particular feeling. For example, if you wake up in the morning feeling anxious, and immediately begin to dread having to deal with your tasks for the day, Barrett suggests that you take a step back and ask yourself what could be causing the anxious feeling. If you're hungry, perhaps addressing that gives your brain a different take on anxiety, and maybe you can tackle your to-do list from a different emotional state than one of dread.

Watch the TEDTalk: *You Aren't at the Mercy of Your Emotions*
—Your Brain Creates Them
(https://c4c.link/13A)

Emotional correctness—in contrast to political correctness—is the tone and the feeling of *how* we say things, more than simply choosing the correct labels or words. Sally Kohn uses her experience as a progressive, lesbian anchor at Fox News to explore this distinction. Because of her views and her identity, she receives a lot of hate mail from people who do not agree with her or who see her identity as unacceptable. When people call her mean and offensive names, she does not care about the words that they are using, but cares about how they use them. Are they being friendly? Naive? Hurtful?

If we want people to understand our point of view, we need to start with respect and compassion. Any hope of continued conversation must begin with a willingness to hear the other person, which happens when we begin with emotional correctness. As Kohn says, "our challenge is to find the compassion for others that we want them to have for us." The *way* that we speak to each other can start conversations that lead to positive change.

Watch the TEDTalk: *Let's Try Emotional Correctness*
(https://c4c.link/13B)

Anger

EMOTIONAL

Awareness Practice
Notice Dislike

Become aware of aversion, the arising of negative feelings toward something or someone. These could be mild feelings, such as irritation, or strong feelings, such as anger or hatred. Try to see what happened just before the aversion arose. What impressions occurred—sights, sounds, touch, taste, smell? Pay attention to when aversion first arises during the day.

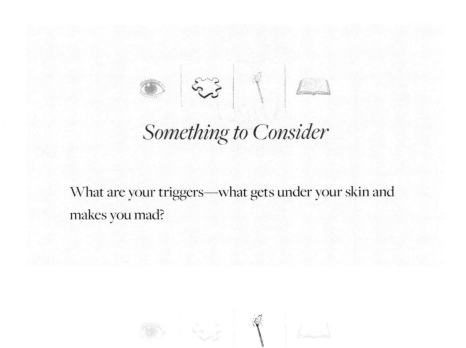

Something to Consider

What are your triggers—what gets under your skin and makes you mad?

Prompts

1) What is something that used to make you mad and now doesn't?

2) Tell about a time when you made someone angry.

Resources

How do you let go of anger that seems so justified? Conversely, what will it cost you to continue to carry it? Folk-rock musician Bhi Bhiman—a guest on a recent podcast with Dacher Keltner—agreed to try a "happiness practice" designed to help one let go of anger. The descendant of Sri Lankan immigrants, Bhiman comes from a people who are no strangers to anger. Tens of thousands of the Tamil people he comes from have been killed in civil war, and Bhiman talks about friends and family who are "eaten away" by the anger they carry. In the practice he agreed to try, Bhiman tackled a simpler anger at one person: a fellow musician who had had an argument with another friend.

Researcher Charlotte van Oyen-Witvliet, a psychology professor at Hope College in Michigan, described the research behind this practice. She asked a group of people to ruminate on a hurtful time for which they continue to feel anger at someone. Half the group were then asked to suppress their negative emotions, while the other half were asked to think about the person who angered them with compassion. At the end, each wrote about the experience and what they'd noticed, and all during the experiment, data was obtained on their heart rates and facial muscle contraction.

During the initial rumination, participants reported intense negative feelings, and sensors detected increased heart rate and tension in muscles under the eyes (consistent with intensity) and in the brow (seen with negative emotions.) Those who suppressed emotion reported less perception of negative emotions, and their heart rates decreased and the facial tension subsided. However, those who activated compassion went beyond simply a loss of negative consequences; in addition to the same results noted in the suppression group, the compassion group reported positive emotions and the muscles associated with smiling were activated.

Furthermore, these participants actually reported feeling empathy for the person they'd been angry with, and difficulty maintaining as many negative thoughts about them. Bhiman described the rapid shift this compassion-based practice brought about in him, saying that the raw, pointy, sharp, intense feelings he had for this former friend seemed smoothed over. And while he didn't say he forgave him, he felt that there was room for them to meet and for a confrontation to potentially be productive, perhaps even eventually leading to forgiveness.

Listen to the podcast: *How to Let Go of Anger*
(https://c4c.link/14A)

On September 21, 2001, in a minimart in Dallas, a Bangladeshi immigrant was asked by a tattooed white man, "Where are you from?" His accented answer bought him a face-full of buckshot. Lying nearly dead on the floor, he vowed to God that if he survived he would live the rest of his life serving mankind. He survived, only to lose his fiancé, his job, his home, and to find himself with $60,000 of debt from medical bills.

In a recent TED Talk, Anand Giridharadas, son of Indian immigrants, speaks of his return to the US, after six years in India, to find a country divided into a Republic of Dreams and a Republic of Fears. A writer, Giridharadas heard of this Bangladeshi man and his attacker and decided to tell their story. After even more hardships, the Bangladeshi immigrant finally held a prestigious job at a blue-chip tech firm, but despite his successes, he realized that among some people born American these same opportunities he'd fought so hard for were simply not realizable. Such was the case with his attacker, who after two other shootings of immigrants in 2001 was now on death row. Raised by a drug-addicted father, sent to subpar schools, told by his mother that she'd been $50 away from aborting him, he first went to prison before he reached puberty.

But on death row he found a new life, visited by caring people and surrounded by positive influences. He came to regret his swastika tattoo upon reading of the Holocaust. He learned that his Bangladeshi victim had sued the state of Texas to stay his execution and was fighting for his pardon. The effort was unsuccessful and he was put to death by lethal injection. But, soon thereafter, his daughter—herself drug-addicted and a convict—received a call from this Bangladeshi man who said, "Though you've lost a father, you've gained an uncle," and pledged to help her. How might we—how might you—create a more merciful country?

Watch the TEDTalk: *Do Hateful People Deserve Forgiveness?*
(https://c4c.link/14B)

Gratitude

EMOTIONAL

Awareness Practice
Appreciation

Stop throughout the day and consciously identify something you appreciate in this moment. It could be a thing you see or hear, an aspect of yourself, or another person who supports you in some way. Be curious, asking yourself, "Is there anything I can appreciate right now?"

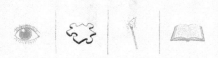

Something to Consider

What are some of the things you appreciate that you've never thanked anyone for?

Prompts

1) Tell about a time you felt thankful but did not say anything.

2) What are the ways you express gratitude?

Resources

Scientists are studying how being thankful can improve your mental health. Many studies have shown that people who consciously practice gratitude are less likely to be depressed. However, most of these studies focus on people who already report normal levels of happiness and have overall good mental health. New studies on people who are struggling with mental health are also showing that writing letters of gratitude to people in their lives is helping their mental health improve beyond counseling alone.

Researchers at Indiana University found some interesting insights suggesting what might underlie the psychological benefits of gratitude. First, gratitude can help us disconnect from toxic emotions. People who wrote letters of gratitude to others used fewer negative words in their writing than those who wrote letters simply about their feelings.

Secondly, gratitude can help even if you don't share it. Most of the participants in the study did not even send their letters to the intended recipients, yet still reported improved mental health effects.

A third finding of their research was that the benefits of gratitude do not come instantly. Participants in the study reported better mental health four weeks after writing letters of gratitude, and then even better results twelve weeks after. The gap in mental health improvement between participants who both practiced gratitude and participated in counseling sessions and those who just did counseling sessions also grew from four weeks to twelve weeks.

Finally, the researchers found that gratitude can have long lasting positive effects on the brain. Three months after the study began, the researchers scanned the brains of people who practiced gratitude and people who didn't while performing a task. They found that the participants who practiced gratitude showed more activation in the part of the brain where learning and decision making happens.

Read the article: *How Gratitude Changes You and Your Brain*
(https://c4c.link/15A)

Brother David Steindl-Rast is a Benedictine monk, an author, and an expert on gratitude. Growing up during World War I and II and being a teenager under Hitler's rule in Austria changed the way he saw the world. After living under such harsh conditions, he became interested in the idea of gratitude and how we can practice it even in the toughest of times. His philosophy is that you cannot be grateful for everything that comes your way, but you can be grateful for every moment. In practice, this means seeing every moment as a new opportunity. The death of a loved one, for example, is not something to be grateful for, but gratitude can be found even in tragedy.

Steindl-Rast's three steps to finding gratitude are simple: stop, look, and go. We as a people are always moving so quickly: rushing, bustling, staying on schedule. The first step is to simply stop for a moment. Next, we have to look. In each moment there is an opportunity to look around and find that window. The last step is to seize the moment. Once we find an opportunity, we need to go do something with it. Joy will follow. As Steindl-Rast points out, there is an important distinction between joy and happiness. Happiness is not steady; joy can be. You can be unhappy yet joyful; you can find inner peace even in deep sadness. Steindl-Rast often says that joy is the "happiness that does not depend on what happens." Joy also favors quality over quantity. There are many moments when our "bowls" fill up with gratitude; we feel so much love and thankfulness for everything we have in our lives, big and small. However, our culture is so competitive that we never let our bowls overflow—we keep making them bigger and bigger so that we can never truly be satisfied with what we have. We look to our neighbors and friends to see what they have that we don't have.

Steindl-Rast is often asked how we can continue to practice gratitude even when there is so much sadness and anxiety in the world. But he sees anxiety as a natural part of life and a beginning rather than an end. We can acknowledge our anxiety without fearing it. When we begin to see anxiety as an opportunity and then avail ourselves of that opportunity, we can move past the fear that paralyzes us.

Listen to the podcast: *How to Be Grateful in Every Moment (But Not for Everything* (https://c4c.link/15B)

Empathy

EMOTIONAL

Awareness Practice
Study Suffering

As you go about your day, pay attention to those who are suffering. How does it show up in you, in others? Where is it most obvious? What are more subtle forms of suffering?

Something to Consider

What keeps you up at night? What tugs at your heart?

Prompts

1) Talk about time you really wanted to be understood by someone. Were you?

2) When have you heard someone else's story and felt it as your own?

Resources

Brené Brown is an author, researcher and university professor who focuses on how we experience courage, vulnerability, shame, and empathy. Brown helps to draw distinctions between empathy, which relates to how we take the position of another and try to see things from their perspective, and sympathy, which is more about feeling bad for someone who is suffering.

Brown says that "empathy fuels connection, while sympathy drives disconnection." Empathy is about recognition and is non-judgmental. Empathy asks us to be with another's suffering; making space and listening. Sympathy, according to Brown, fails to take us outside of our own experience of suffering and tends to be less effective in actually helping ease someone else's pain. While empathy does not attempt to fix another person's suffering, it is often an effective way to build relationship and offers some space and regard, which can be helpful as someone we care about works through their pain. This is often just what is needed when someone is experiencing grief or suffering. A further distinction might be made between empathy and compassion, which involves empathy, as well as a commitment to serve the situation in a way that eases suffering for all involved.

Read the article: *The Power of Empathy*
(and One Surefire Way to Know If You're Missing it)
(https://c4c.link/16A)

Sharon Salzberg is a world-renowned author and teacher of meditation, mindfulness and lovingkindness. She argues that we often allow anger to block our capacity to feel empathy, but that there are practices that enable us to turn from anger toward love. She offers classes and shares self-intervention practices that encourage us to first recognize anger, then really consider the situation in which it arises and what, if anything, might be done to help improve the situation (including, perhaps, stepping away from it). She encourages us to use gratitude and to recognize that understanding and acceptance (even of our experience of anger) can be an act of compassion. Salzberg suggests we become a student of the arising and dissipating of anger, as well as all the other emotions we experience. She suggests we can actually "alchemize" anger into some act of love.

Read the article: *From Anger to Love: The Art of Self-Intervention*
(https://c4c.link/16B)

Happiness

EMOTIONAL

Awareness Practice
Giving a Gift of Kindness

Pick one person and offer one thing that might be appreciated, a greeting, a check in, a thank you, a pat on the back. Try to imagine what might bring that person joy, laughter, pleasure. Focus on the experience of giving, in person.

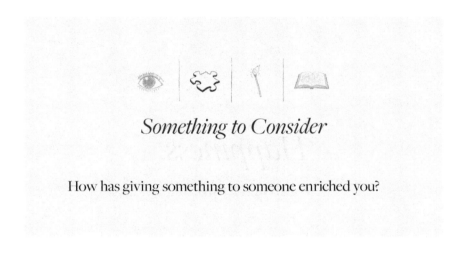

Something to Consider

How has giving something to someone enriched you?

Prompts

1) Recall and describe a time in your life that you were really happy.

2) Who is a person you know that seems to be happy a lot—why might that be so?

Resources

Everyone agrees that in life we all want happiness. Buddhist monk Matthieu Ricard believes that we can train our minds in the habit of wellbeing, which can lead to lasting happiness. The distinction between happiness and pleasure is important. Pleasure is fleeting and conditional: for example, a delicious chocolate cake when you're hungry can bring a lot of both happiness and pleasure. But, once you've eaten half the cake, you reach the point where chocolate cake is disgusting. Similarly with a song you love: the first time you hear it, it's an amazing experience and you believe you will be happy if only you can hear it over again. But, if you listen to it a thousand times in a row, you're going to start to hate it. The pleasurable feeling doesn't last.

True happiness, Matthieu Ricard says, is not dependent on conditions. In searching for happiness, we tend to look outwards, gathering material goods. We believe that we need things to be happy, and if we don't have one of those things, our happiness collapses. The attempt to create perfect conditions for happiness dooms us from ever realizing it as our control of the outer world is extremely limited. Instead, we must turn inward if we want to find happiness. Ricard's key to nurturing lasting happiness begins with training our minds, and is more simple than you might think. We begin with shining the light of awareness on what we are feeling in each moment.

Certain emotions, like anger, jealousy, or hatred, lead us away from happiness. Other emotions like love, or actions like selfless generosity, leave us with a good feeling. Ultimately, though, all emotions are fleeting, and so there is always a possibility for change. With training in mindfulness, we see that we are not constantly in a state of anger, jealousy, generosity, or affection. Paradoxically, it is in the letting go of both aversion to feeling one way and clinging to feeling another that allows for deep and lasting happiness. Rather than magic or some new scientific breakthrough, it is as simple as getting to know your own mind.

Watch the TEDTalk: *The Habits of Happiness*
(https://c4c.link/17A)

Happiness is very difficult to measure. Does money buy happiness? Does love? The World Happiness Report ranks all the countries in the world each year. In 2019, the United States ranked 19th, behind Belgium, Australia, Israel, Canada, and others. The happiest country in the world, Finland, might actually be the happiest because of how little they value rankings and comparison! John Helliwell, a leading economist, says that in Finland, it's a social norm to not display or talk about how much money you have: Finns don't buy a lot of things that show others their wealth.

The World Happiness Report uses six measures of happiness: GDP per capita (the sum total of all the goods and services a country produces in a year per person), life expectancy, how much people trust the government and business in their country, how much social support a person has, generosity (whether or not a person has helped someone out in the last 30 days), and freedom. The factors that seem the best predictors of happiness are social support and GDP per capita. This means that countries where people have big social networks and countries where the people are richer are more likely to be happier countries. The few exceptions to this are China, India, and the United States: these are all countries where even though the GDP is increasing, happiness is decreasing.

This is probably because of the Easterlin Paradox: the idea, proven by economists, that shows that wealth affects happiness only up to a certain point. People in the US, China, and India tend to overestimate the happiness they gain from receiving a higher income and underestimate the happiness they lose from spending less time with family due to more time spent working and commuting. So while having all the money in the world does not buy happiness, perhaps having *enough* money can make someone happier. Nonetheless, prioritizing time for family and friends gives us a better shot at being happy in the long run.

Listen to the podcast: *How to Measure Happiness*
(https://c4c.link/17B)

Vulnerability

EMOTIONAL

Awareness Practice
Use Your Non-Dominant Hand

Use your non-dominant hand for some ordinary task today. This could be brushing your teeth, combing your hair, or eating with the non-dominant hand for at least part of a meal. If you're up for a big challenge, try using the non-dominant hand when writing.

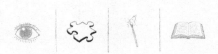

Something to Consider

When you think about people with disabilities, what do you think they have to do to accomplish simple tasks?

Prompts

1) Tell a story about a time you took a risk.

2) Tell about a time your vulnerability had an effect on another person, or theirs had an effect on you.

Resources

Connection is what makes the world go round. In her TED Talk, Brené Brown talks about the power of vulnerability. For us to be able to have true connections with other people, we need to allow ourselves to be seen. Brown talks about how people who struggle to be vulnerable are insecure about their worthiness, their sense of belonging and acceptance. People who are able to be vulnerable have a strong sense of worthiness, and because of their courage, they experience compassion and connection with others. Brown describes this courage as the ability to tell the story of who you are with your whole heart and risk being imperfect. She emphasizes that we have to practice compassion with ourselves in order to be able give it to others.

In order to make connections, we need to embrace vulnerability as well as that which makes us authentically who we are. Brown knows that being vulnerable is not comfortable, and brings no guarantees for connection, but she emphasizes that vulnerability can be the place where love is created, where we find belonging and acceptance of ourselves. Brown says that you can't only numb shame, blame, sadness and disappointment without also numbing joy, happiness, and goodness. Seeing people in our lives, as well as ourselves, as imperfect but worthy of love allows all to be seen, which is the place from which connection happens.

Watch the TEDTalk: *The Power of Vulnerability*
(https://c4c.link/18A)

Sharing your weaknesses with others is the best way to develop trust. Jeff Polzer, a professor of organizational behavior at Harvard, says that vulnerability is about "sending a clear signal that you have weaknesses" and that you could use some help. By setting this example, you allow room for people to share their own weaknesses despite their insecurities. Polzer says that vulnerability has to be a two-way street; if the person who you being vulnerable towards refuses to show you their own weaknesses or pretends they don't have any, then it won't work.

Daniel Coyle calls this back and forth willingness to be open about your short-comings the "vulnerability loop," which he says is the most basic building block of cooperation and trust. Contrary to what we often think (that we have to first trust each other before we can be vulnerable), vulnerability actually comes before trust. Coyle says that if we jump into the unknown with other people, then we will land with each other on a solid ground made of trust. He describes a test designed by DARPA (Defense Advanced Research Project Agency), a group within the U.S. Department of Defense which has the responsibility of preparing the U.S. military for technological issues in the future.

In this test, which they called the Red Balloon Challenge, DARPA hid ten balloons over a 3.1 million square mile radius and said that the first group to find all ten balloons would win $40,000. MIT's Media Lab set up a team only days before the release, which meant they couldn't prepare a lot. Through an online website they told people that if they helped find the balloon, they would win a certain amount of money as would anyone else who helped them win the competition. Because of this guarantee, MIT was able to get a lot of people to sign up for the search and ended up winning the competition only a few hours after it started. Other teams sent out messages to people saying that they "might" win money, and did not give people a lot of guarantees. The author says MIT won because they asked for people's vulnerability and gave their own vulnerability back to them. Other teams asked for participant's vulnerability without being vulnerable themselves. Overall, cooperation and trust was built on mutual vulnerability and proved beneficial to everyone involved.

Watch the TEDTalk: *How Showing Vulnerability Helps Build a Stronger Team*
(https://c4c.link/18B)

Social & Energetic Awareness

Finally, we turn toward *social and energetic awareness*: what are we really curious about that is intangible? What do we do with "the elephant in the room" before it is named? How do we understand the interactions and relationships between ourselves and those around us? What does it mean to empathize or to forge a bond, and how do our relationships change our experience of life, culture, systems, community?

Social & Energetic Awareness

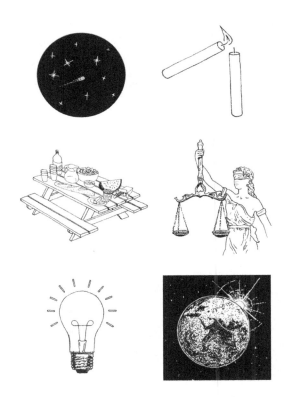

Insight

SOCIAL & ENERGETIC

Awareness Practice
Looking Deeply Into Food

When you eat, take a moment to look into the food or drink as if you could see backward, into its history. Use the power of imagination to see where it came from and how many people might have been involved in bringing it to you, from the inception of the ingredients to the moment you eat or drink. Send some gratitude to those people and other living beings before you take a sip or a bite.

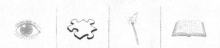

Something to Consider

How far have all of the ingredients in the food you eat today travelled and who are the people, animals and plants that have had something to do with your ability to eat today?

Prompts

1) What lesson that you learned as a child stays with you and shows up in your life in some way today?

2) What qualities do you think your friends value in you?

Resources

Telling a story from only one point of view can leave the listener with a skewed view of reality. This is what Chimamanda Ngozi Adichie calls the "danger of a single story." Adichie talks about growing up in a middle class family in the West African country of Nigeria. Her father was a professor and her mother an administrator, but having only British and American books growing up, Adichie thought only blond-haired, blue-eyed kids showed up in books and did not realize that she could read and write about people who looked like her.

Coming to the United States for university, she was stereotyped by her roommate, who knew only a single story of what Africa was like: wild animals, people dying from disease and starvation, and Bedouins on camels in the desert. The roommate never saw Africa as being similar to where she grew up, and didn't see African people as being like her because that was not how they were shown to her.

But far from only being the recipient of stereotyping, Adichie admits to her own limited views when she talks about traveling to Guadalajara, Mexico, and how what she saw challenged her bias that all Mexicans are immigrants. When she saw them going to work, laughing, in community together she realized that she had only had a single story for Mexican people before that moment. Telling only one story of a people over and over again makes it the only story by which they are known. Adichie encourages us to move past stereotypes and the tendency to "make one story become the only story" into a place of seeing others as worthy of dignity and maybe more similar to us than we think.

Watch the TEDTalk: *The Danger of a Single Story*
(https://c4c.link/19A)

Experiencing a high amount of trauma as a child affects brain development, the immune system, hormonal systems and even impacts DNA. Dr. Nadine Burke Harris talks about how after opening a clinic in Bayview-Hunters Point, one of the most underserved neighborhoods in San Francisco, she realized that most of the children she was serving had extremely high exposures to "adverse childhood experiences" (ACEs). These experiences include "physical, emotional, or sexual abuse, physical or emotional neglect, parental mental illness, substance dependence, incarceration" and many other traumatic events.

Through a study conducted by two doctors in the 90s, it was discovered that ACEs were extremely common. In the study, they also found that people with more ACEs had worse health outcomes. Exposure to these experiences at such a young age can affect areas in our brains that are in charge of our impulse control and executive functioning (critical areas for learning), our flight or fight response, and the pleasure and reward center of the brain, to name a few. People with many ACEs are more likely to engage in high risk behaviors, like drinking or drugs, because of these changes in their brains.

However, Harris mentions that even if you don't engage in high risk behaviors, you are still more likely to have worse health outcomes if you have ACEs. She says this is because repeated stress in children affects brain structure and function and leads to poor health when the body's flight or fight response is activated over and over again. Mental health care, nutrition, and education about the impacts of ACEs and toxic stress are a few of the ways that we can address these poor outcomes, and she stresses that this problem is treatable.

Watch the TEDTalk: *How Childhood Trauma Affects Health Across a Lifetime*
(https://c4c.link/19B)

Compassion

SOCIAL & ENERGETIC

Awareness Practice
Secret Acts of Virtue

Today and the next three days, engage in a secret act of virtue or kindness. Do something nice or needed for others, but do so anonymously. This can be very simple, such as saying a prayer, wishing the person well or offering a word of encouragement.

Something to Consider

What impact does it have on others when you give them something that's not a thing (time, attention, words, etc.)?

Prompts

1) Tell of a time you did the right thing for someone, despite challenges.

2) Describe a time you received or experienced an unexpected kindness from someone.

Resources

Compassion may be thought of as a "moral emotion" that moves us to care for and attend to the suffering of others and can lead us to create more cooperative and harmonious relationships. As a result of a barrage of media images of the suffering of others, we can experience an overload or fatigue that causes us to shrink away.

C. Daryl Cameron, an assistant professor of social psychology at the University of Iowa argues that we can expand our "compassion bandwidth" without causing ourselves harm. Cameron's research focuses on the causes and consequences of compassion, and on how emotions influence moral decisions. He observes that, while people anticipate that they would feel more compassion for the suffering of more people, in fact the opposite is true.

In Cameron's research, people associate a greater cost (financially, emotionally) to the suffering of a greater number of people and they fear that they will not be capable of making a difference and will quickly become fatigued, causing their compassion toward a larger group to diminish. He argues that compassion does not so much disappear as it is actively turned off by people who assess it to not be practical or worthwhile. Teaching skills of self-care and sustained attention, as well as addressing fears of the cost of compassion, leads to people expanding their compassion bandwidth, Cameron asserts. Qualities developed in mindfulness practice, like sustaining focus on the present moment and non-judging also reinforce the ability to increase compassion.

At a time when skillfulness and commitment to compassion for others is so needed in the world, Cameron believes that training in mindfulness may be an important component of increasing individual capacity to attend to and help ease widespread, as well as individual, suffering.

Read the article: *How to Increase Your Compassion Bandwidth*
(https://c4c.link/20A)

Christopher Bergland is science writer and public health advocate who has a background as an ultra-endurance athlete. Bergland asserts that recent neuro-scientific studies demonstrate the way in which meditation and other mindfulness practices transform our brains and cultivate concentration, empathy and insight—and how these practices are an effective and important tool in the world right now, to combat violence, aggression and suffering. Bergland describes the Dalai Lama's response to widespread incidents of violence and his emphasis on the versatility and flexibility of meditation practices, practices grounded in Buddhism, but adaptable throughout the world and across cultures.

In order to cultivate world peace, Bergland quotes the Dalai Lama as saying, "we need to take a more secular, rather than a religious, approach to fostering ethics." Bergland cites research on positive growth in brain regions associated with empathy as a result of subjects practicing compassion meditation. Research conducted by University of Wisconsin Professor Richard Davidson, and others, demonstrates the plasticity of our brains and how, utilizing meditative practices, we can build up brain structures and functionality that support and promote greater happiness and compassion for others.

The research suggests that individuals, as well as society in general could benefit greatly from meditative practices. Training in compassion has a range of benefits, including preventing depression, enhancing health and resilience, improving relationships and building community. Teaching mindfulness practices to children holds the promise of decreasing bullying, aggression and violence. Davidson and others are exploring effective ways to scale these practices for children, including developing mindfulness-influenced video games.

Bergland also discusses recent studies that indicate the specific impact of different types of meditation training on the development of different areas and functionality of the brain, including the way we experience emotions, as well as our stress regulation. A variety of meditation practices seem to result in enduring, beneficial changes in brain function, especially in the area of emotional processing. But scientists are discovering variations in the impact of different types and styles of meditation.

While mindfulness meditation may emphasize concentration and the ability to attend non-judgmentally to thoughts and feelings, Cognitively-Based Compassion Training, or CBCT, includes a focus on training people to analyze and reinterpret their relationships with others. This approach leans into the idea of interconnectivity and a desire that all beings be free from suffering and leads to different outcomes. Bergland concludes that, as a society and a nation, we must all come together to decrease violence and aggression toward one another and that meditation is proving to be an effective methodology for achieving this.

Read the article: *Mindfulness Training and the Compassionate Brain*
(https://c4c.link/2oB)

Non-judgment

SOCIAL & ENERGETIC

Awareness Practice
Listen Like a Sponge

Choose a few encounters today and listen to soak up everything the person says. Let the mind be quiet, just take it in. Don't formulate any response in the mind until one is requested or needed.

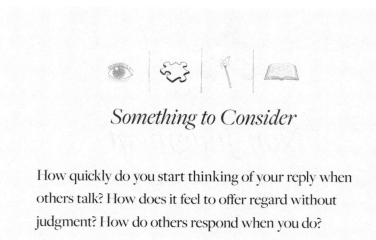

Something to Consider

How quickly do you start thinking of your reply when others talk? How does it feel to offer regard without judgment? How do others respond when you do?

Prompts

1) Tell the story of a time you felt fully seen and valued.

2) What is something you have avoided really seeing or someone you refuse to listen to?

Resources

Elliott Dacher, MD, writes about non-judgment as a "healing elixir." He posits that nonjudgment is an act of kindness and compassion we perform toward ourselves and others. Our lives are made up of prioritizations and choices and it may seem as if we are constantly judging, analyzing, sorting, choosing. Dacher describes a sorting of experience into the things we like and those we don't, the pleasurable and the unpleasurable.

We spend our lives, he writes, striving toward and grasping for half of existence and rejecting and running away from the other half. Our judgments, he writes, are "suffering in disguise." He asks us to imagine walking through an arboretum and deciding which plants we would like for our garden—it is not necessary, he asserts, to decide that one plant is *better* than another to choose it. He suggests that we consider encountering and interacting with things as they are, not accepting or rejecting, agreeing or disagreeing—just encountering things and making choices that are right for us without passing judgment on the thing we are choosing or not choosing. We can appreciate something without it being the thing we choose.

This attitude gives us the opportunity for "a lovely appreciation and gratitude for the diversity of life and people." Dacher suggests we try this non-judgment, as an exercise, for a short period of time—accepting things we encounter as they are. He suggests we try this in nature, when listening to another person, when speaking our mind. Dacher suggests that our meditation practice is a great place to work on non-judgment, meeting thoughts, feelings, mental images as they arise, noticing them, and watching them fall away. (This practice feels to be very much what is practiced when we sit in council, speaking and listening "from the heart.") Non-judgment is trustworthy, reliable, and always available, and it has the ability to calm an overactive mind and quiet disturbing emotions.

Read the article: *The Power of Non-Judgment*
(https://c4c.link/21A)

Joey Fung, Ph.D., is an Associate Professor of Psychology at Fuller Theological Seminary. She writes about our constant thought-stream and the chatter of inner dialogue we run, around how we respond to and come to understand the experiences we have. We often play out justifications and reasoning around our "rightness" and the justification we have for feeling aggrieved, slighted, wronged by adverse experiences or antagonistic people. This often involves a self-justification around our personal perspective and narrative, a myopic interpretation of events that seldom leaves room for the diversity of perspectives that might be possible around an experience we have had.

Fung urges us to mind that gap between an experience and our thought about the experience. "As I create distance from my thoughts," she writes, "I create space within myself. I become less reactive, and more thoughtful. And I can live more fully in the present moment." Our thoughts, then, are not who we are—and we can create the space that enables us to move toward or away from our thoughts, aligned with our ethical base.

Fung gives an example of a monk who has lustful thoughts. The monk is not a bad person, but he may observe the thought and choose not to act on it, as it is not aligned with his path or the vows he has chosen to live by. He can acknowledge his thoughts and refrain from judging himself, and he can also evaluate whether the thought is consistent with his moral compass. He does not beat himself up or consider himself a failure—but he works with the thought and incorporates it into his decision-making, allowing the thought to be part of the sense-making and definition of his action, even if that action will be taken in opposition to what the thought presents. Mindfulness encourages us to connect with our deeper purpose, values and meaning, Fung concludes. And that is only possible if we are honest, attentive and include all experiences, without judging as unworthy, rejecting or dismissing anything out of hand.

Read the article: *The Role of Nonjudgment in Mindfulness*
(https://c4c.link/21B)

Community

SOCIAL & ENERGETIC

Awareness Practice
True Compliments

Think of someone close to you—a family member, or friend—and write a letter in which you offer a genuine compliment, the more specific the compliment, the better. Also become aware of any compliments other people give you. Investigate the purpose of compliments and their effect on you.

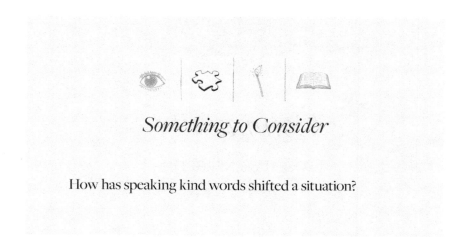

Something to Consider

How has speaking kind words shifted a situation?

Prompts

1) How does it feel to be with your people?

2) Tell about a time you were "a fish out of water."

Resources

Sally Kohn, a political commentator and author, has always been told that she's a "nice person." But at one point, she remembered a time when she wasn't so nice. In fifth grade, she tormented one of her classmates named Vicki; Vicki had hygiene problems and Sally called her "Sticky Vicki." Being the recipient of hate mail in her work, as well as recalling her own hateful behavior, Kohn decided to take a deeper look at why we hate others. She traveled around the world, from Rwanda to the Middle East to across the United States, studying different forms of hate. From war and genocide to thinking that your ingroup is better than another outgroup, she concluded that it is all the same hate, just on different levels.

Kohn found during her investigation that everyone agrees that hate is bad and is fundamentally against it. But at the same time, everyone hates. We justify hating people because we think they hate us. At the root of hate is the idea that we are fundamentally good and they are fundamentally bad. Kohn did find glimmers of hope, however, in some of the most extreme situations.

While in the Middle East, she met Bassam Aramin, who at 16 years old attempted to bomb an Israeli military base. While in prison, he was forced to watch a documentary about the Holocaust (which he had previously been told was a myth). Learning about the truth of the Holocaust changed him; after prison he got a master's degree in Holocaust studies and founded an organization for Palestinian and Israeli combatants to come together and try to make peace.

Studies show that we don't come into this world with hate, it is learned and becomes ingrained by society. The first step to unlearning hate has to come from recognizing the hate we hold in all forms. Integration is also incredibly important to curbing hate: preschoolers who attend integrated schools hold fewer biases into adulthood. Years later, Sally was eventually able to track down Vicki. She wrote an apology letter asking Vicki to forgive her. Vicki offered her conditional forgiveness: she challenged Sally to end the cycle of hate, by going out into the world to prevent others from acting like she did.

Watch the TEDTalk: *What Is The Opposite Of Hate?*
(https://c4c.link/22A)

When Rhonda Magee, JD, became a tenured professor, the dean of her law school sent her flowers. When the flower delivery man came to the door and asked for Professor Magee, he was shocked and did not believe that the petite Black woman dressed simply in front of him was the professor. Even though he was a Black man himself, he still held the belief that a Black woman could not be a professor of law.

These deeply held beliefs are called "implicit biases" and we all have them. When we hear words like "professor," we get a mental picture of what that person ought to look like. The consequences of implicit bias can be very dangerous; in the criminal justice system, implicit bias can lead to the death of innocent people. Practicing mindfulness can help us focus, control our emotions, and think clearly and act purposefully.

Researchers looking for ways to reduce racial bias have found that mindfulness can also help police and other public servants reduce biases that lead to inflicting harm on innocent people. And it doesn't require that one be a long-time meditator: a very brief mindfulness practice reduced race and age bias on the Implicit Attitude Test, a test that measures how much implicit bias a person holds.

In the past 40 years, the way that racism shows up has changed a lot. A new kind of racism, which scholars have coined "colorblind racism," has come out of a new push to not see color. By pretending that our differences don't exist, we have allowed racism to continue in both overt and subtle forms. Magee wanted to study how mindfulness could reduce racial bias, but she wanted to make sure that the practice wasn't colorblind. She created a methodology called "ColorInsight" which combines mindfulness with learning about race and color to create the opportunity for deeper understanding and awareness of how we are impacted by these issues. The goal of ColorInsight Practice is not only to reduce our implicit biases but also to create better cross-race relationships in a society. This work holds a lot of potential to create change not only on a person-to-person level but also in systems like policing.

Read the article: *How Mindfulness Can Defeat Racial Bias*
(https://c4c.link/22B)

Awe

SOCIAL & ENERGETIC

Awareness Practice
Appreciate Not Knowing

Throughout this week, notice small moments that surprise you or force you to look again, to rethink or reset. Notice when you are on autopilot and as you snap back into the present moment.

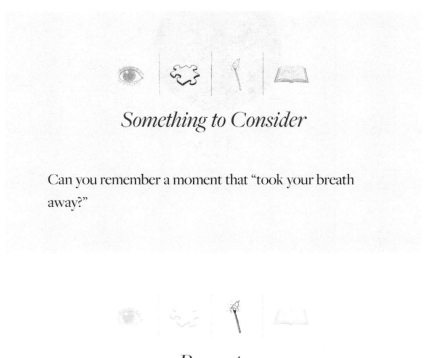

Something to Consider

Can you remember a moment that "took your breath away?"

Prompts

1) Tell about someone (living, dead or imaginary) who inspires you or someone who has had your back.

2) Tell a story about something that was truly awesome or that stopped you dead in your tracks.

Resources

Dacher Keltner, a professor of psychology who studies the experience of awe, describes it as a state that is beyond one's current frame of reference. When you're in a state of awe, you cannot intellectualize what is happening because it is beyond your current base of knowledge. Awe can come from natural sources, like seeing a grand cascading waterfall, or it can come from manmade sources, like music or art.

Michael Pollan, an author, journalist, and professor, has studied the relationship between awe and psychedelics extensively. He believes that awe and the self are in an oppositional relationship with one another. Fear is also part of awe. It may not be one of the feelings we associate most with listening to a beautiful piece of music that leaves us speechless, but even in this experience, fear is present. When we are in awe, we are opened up to the unknown. Threatened and exposed, fear can be the vehicle by which awe becomes transformational.

Deep awe can also come acting in service of others or experiencing the death of a loved one. People in the world today are more self-focused and anxious than ever before. A global survey conducted by researchers found that people self-report having only two experiences of awe per week. About 10% of the time those experiences of awe come from ourselves. All in all, we could all benefit from having more experiences in our lives that leave us in a state of awe.

Watch the video: *The Power of Awe*

(https://c4c.link/23A)

Pico Iyer has always dreamed of traveling the world. As soon as he was old enough to work, he did odd jobs wherever he could in order to make enough money to achieve that goal, and eventually became a travel writer. But when he was 29 years old, deep in the midst of what he thought was his dream life, he realized that something was missing.

Like many other people in this fast-paced, socially demanding era, he wasn't taking any time to stop and think about his life. He ended up abandoning his dream life and moved to a single room on the backstreets of Kyoto, Japan where he had no car, bicycle, TV, or cell phone. He still lives there and rarely ever checks the time; he has come to realize that time spent going nowhere is much more valuable than all the time spent traveling around the world.

In this day and age where the world around us never seems to stop asking us to *do*, Iyer suggests we could all benefit from more *doing nothing*. Sociologists found that even though we are actually working less hours than we did 50 years ago, we feel like we are working more. We have more time saving devices but less time. The people who invented the devices that now dictate our lives know best how damaging they can be.

That is why many people who work at Google or Apple or Microsoft take something called an "Internet Sabbath"—each week, they completely log off from all devices for 24–48 hours. When you sit completely still you find out what moves you most. You can make sense of the past and the future and remind yourself of where you want to be going. So much of our life takes place in our heads; if we want to change our lives, we need to change our minds. Changing your mind begins with being most in touch with it and being disconnected from the rest of the world.

Watch the TEDTalk: *The Art of Stillness*

(https://c4c.link/23B)

Beyond Us & Them

SOCIAL & ENERGETIC

Awareness Practice
Othering

This week, notice who you "other." Make a list of who you consider "us" and who you consider "them"—who is in your club? When meeting someone new, notice your own sense of like/dislike, trust/distrust, attraction/aversion. Consider what it takes for you to rethink the group you assigned someone to be in.

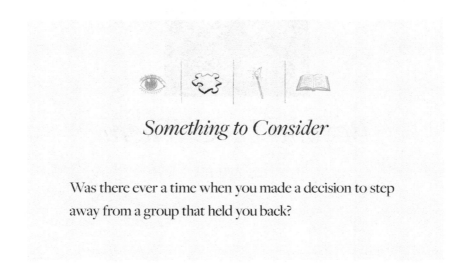

Something to Consider

Was there ever a time when you made a decision to step away from a group that held you back?

Prompts

1) Who is someone you thought was one thing, but realized later was more than you had thought?

2) If there were no pressures or there would be no repercussions, who would you want to get to know a bit better?

Resources

Educators, activists, formerly incarcerated individuals, and police officers, all having been trained in the practice of council within their own groups, came together in September of 2018 for a daylong workshop. Each person came bravely but also with caution and the question, "What happens when we bring all these groups into one council circle together?"

For Sofia, a community activist, council was a rare space where everyone was on equal ground, and where each person's voice was equally important. Sam, who was incarcerated for 17 years, found that council transformed his life; as he and other participants told each other their stories, and realized that they shared a lot of the same experiences, he felt less alone. For Gena, a lieutenant with the LAPD, council was a therapeutic way to unpack all of the things she saw on the job that stayed with her.

Still, participants felt trepidation when they first encountered each other. Before the council session began, the tension in the room was palpable. Community activists were nervous at the presence of the police and the police were aware that people were apprehensive of them. No one hid their discomfort. Each participant brought a different viewpoint.

As the day unfolded, however, and the talking piece changed hands, a common theme arose: children. Everyone in the room was either a parent or someone's child, and everyone had stories to share about their relationship with their parents or children. Little sparks of everyone's humanity began to come out.

Ken, a police officer who began the day wary and restrained, was moved in council to share a story about his wife bringing home a pet rabbit that he developed a particular affection for and decided to nickname "Bun Buns." The room erupted with laughter. Ken's sharing this sweet story seemed to warm the hearts of the other participants, even those who had previously been defensive. That broke the ice and, by the end of the session, new relationships started to emerge. Sam and Gena chatted and realized that they shared very similar backgrounds, though they had taken completely different paths in life. Hazel, a teacher, admitted to seeing officers in a new light as a result of their stories in the council. Sam and Ken went on to connect on a deeper level, spurred by a curiosity about what the other had shared in council, and they developed a strong mutual respect for each other. Ken reflected that he had the sense that there are many other formerly incarcerated people just like Sam out there, but he just hadn't had the chance to get to know them yet. Gena reflected that she now believes that everyone needs to sit in council. The feeling at the end of the session was that all who attended had been inspired and transformed by the connections they experienced and the power of council.

Watch the video: *Cops and Communities: Circling Up*
(https://c4c.link/24A)

David DeSteno, a psychology professor aware of the decline in care for the wellbeing of others from 1979–2009, decided to devise a study to see whether people could become more compassionate and empathetic. DeSteno's experiment involved 39 people, all of whom had never meditated before. Half of the group completed an eight-week meditation course led by a Buddhist expert and the other half had no meditation training. After eight weeks, all the participants were invited back to the lab, individually, and told that they would be completing tasks that measure attention and memory.

In reality, the meat of the study took place in the waiting room. There were three chairs in the waiting room, and each participant was seated next to two actors. A third actor entered on crutches, moaning in pain, and leaned against a wall as there was nowhere to sit. The other actors who were sitting down purposefully ignored her distress and continued to scroll through their phones. The researchers wanted to see whether participants would get up and offer their seat to a person in pain.

What they found was incredible. Only 16% of the subjects who never meditated offered their seat. But of the subjects who participated in the meditation course, 50% of the subjects gave up their seat! To verify that it was meditation itself that made the difference (and not the Buddhist expert's involvement), they did the experiment again, but this time with a meditation app. They found a similar startling difference: 37% of meditators gave up their seat compared to 14% who had never meditated before.

Empathy is the experience of feeling another's pain; when we see other people in distress, we may actually feel their pain. For many, the self-protective response is to turn away from the person who is suffering. Researchers who study what happens in our brain when we meditate are finding that meditators do experience the distress of the other, but that this distress occurs briefly, then quickly shifts to thoughts of compassion.

Read the article: *The Kindness Cure*
(https://c4c.link/24B)

Epilogue

If we could change ourselves, the tendencies in the world
would also change. As a man changes his own nature, so
does the attitude of the world change towards him.... We
need not wait to see what others do.

—Mahatma Gandhi

Contemplative traditions throughout history have reminded us that our inward journey to the core of who we are must accompany the outward voyage. Our path moves outward into our lives, as it travels inward toward our hearts. As we practice listening ever more deeply to what it is to be human, we sharpen our tools and build the skills we need to create a life of peace, love and connection, as well as the capacity to be of service and attend to the suffering we encounter in ourselves and others. Coming to know our innermost sensations, thoughts and feelings is a step toward self-compassion. Speaking and listening from the heart, expressing ourselves authentically and listening attentively to others, without judgment, creates the foundation for compassionate action towards others. Listening from the heart represents a critical building block in constructing a life that is meaningful and beneficial. Practicing and embodying mindfulness and council fosters the insight, compassion and skillfulness that is so critically needed in the world right now. As one of the participants in the council program at Mule Creek State Prison wrote recently: "Being 'together' is the heart of our journey, whether with oneself or with others, it builds our soul through time. It is how we find inner peace, together."

I hope this book has supported you on this leg of your journey. You may well find that you return to this very exploration again and again, each time entering a bit deeper and dropping in a bit further. Practicing the skills of listening and speaking from the heart offers a chance to move in the world with resilience and strength, our vulnerability and compassion coupled with resolve and courage. As we train to open our ears, minds, will and hearts, we strengthen our capacity to see and meet the world as it is, and to discern how best to respond. Through this practice, we can transform ourselves and the world around us. And we find the courage to engage and celebrate the many wonders that come our way.

This being human is a guest house.
Every morning a new arrival.

A joy, a depression, a meanness,
some momentary awareness comes
as an unexpected visitor.

Welcome and entertain them all!
Even if they're a crowd of sorrows,
who violently sweep your house
empty of its furniture,
still, treat each guest honorably.
He may be clearing you out
for some new delight.

The dark thought, the shame, the malice,
meet them at the door laughing,
and invite them in.

Be grateful for whoever comes,
because each has been sent
as a guide from beyond.

—Jelaluddin Rumi
"Guest House," translated by
Coleman Barks

Council and the Science of Stress

(Contributed by Dr. Ann Seide—certified council trainer and practicing physician, specializing in integrative medicine and palliative care.)

Welcome to the inside of your nervous system! Throughout this book, you've been introduced to practices of mindfulness and meditation, along with the practice of council. Here, we will take a brief look at what's happening in your nervous system under normal conditions, as well as when it's stressed, to help you better make sense of your body and mind's responses and how you might work with them to create better health.

You may have noticed that when you've tried to sit quietly, thoughts seem to come out of nowhere. Our brains are busy even at rest, creating thoughts like our pancreas secretes insulin. Recalling the past, or imagining the future, back and forth—our minds weave stories of who we were and fantasies of what will be. Even in this (supposedly) relaxed state, we may find ourselves overwhelmed by thoughts, and even emotions and physical sensations (like a racing heart, dry mouth, grumbling stomach.) These sensations are all the result of a nervous system that continually senses and responds to our environment (both internal and external), leading to responses that ideally help us live and thrive.

It's important to understand that stress is not a bad thing, nor is it a problem we must fix; the absence of all stress is not a condition that we should strive to achieve. Stress plays an important role in our ability to understand and respond to messages from our senses, the world in which we live, and the others who make up our communities, families, workplaces. Stress also functions as an important catalyst for our growth and stability. Imagine the salmon deprived of rushing rivers to swim up, or tall palm trees without winds to steady against—or a system of government without any ability for dissent or the balance of competing interests. As we will discuss here, stress plays a critical role in our lives, helping us navigate unexpected challenges that we encounter and nurturing wholesome relationships and community. When unregulated, however, stress has the potential to disrupt our physical health and ability to function in a productive way.

Jon Kabat-Zinn coined the term "Mindfulness Based Stress Reduction" and launched a cultural phenomenon in this country that brought attention to "managing stress" as a practice of wellness. MBSR has introduced many health professionals to the study of stress and has provided a lens through which to explore the many benefits to a healthier physiology accessible through working with contemplative practices like meditation, yoga and council. It has also created a great deal of interest and energy around the scientific study of the characteristics of a healthy nervous system and a biological understanding of the benefits of mitigating habitual stress response and avoiding a chronically dysregulated nervous system.

The Normal Nervous System

Our nervous system is made up of two components: the *voluntary* and the *involuntary*. The voluntary nervous system is under our direct control; it's how we raise a glass to drink, stand up and walk a few steps, hug a loved one. The involuntary (or autonomic) nervous system, on the other hand, largely operates without our needing to consciously direct it, controlling our heart's beat, breathing, digestion. Though we don't need to "think" our heart to beat 80 times per minute, there are things that we consciously do that influence our autonomic responses.

The autonomic nervous system is further divided into two branches. In the *sympathetic* nervous system (SNS), nerves travel from the central nervous system (CNS), or the brain and spinal cord, out into our organs, blood vessels, muscles, and glands. This branch activates the "fight, flight, or freeze" response, causing a rapid heart rate, deep breathing, dry mouth, pupil dilation, and inhibition of digestion. Relatively speaking, it is a fast-conducting pathway composed of two neurons. One particular pathway is super-fast, from the CNS via one neuron connecting directly to the adrenal glands which sit atop our kidneys. In response, these glands will secrete adrenalin and cortisol, which through the blood stream cause an even more pronounced and sustained activating, sympathetic response.

The *parasympathetic* nervous system (PNS), in contrast, causes the "rest, digest, and discern" response. The action of these nerves slow heart rate and breathing, enhance salivation and digestion, and constrict pupils. It is a slower system, also comprised of two neurons—one beginning in the CNS and the other in the target organ. One very important distinction between the PNS and the SNS is that information in the parasympathetic system travels *both ways*. The large nerve that is composed of bundles of parasympathetic fibers—the vagus nerve—is a superhighway of information, coursing back and forth between the brain and the end organs. Impulses from our gut, our heart muscle, even the muscles that hold us upright, all send information about the "state of affairs" within our body back to our brain. And, conversely, our thoughts and conscious enactment of deeper breathing sends information to our organs.

In order to be healthy, we need both aspects of our autonomic nervous system to continually be in flux. There is a constant level of PNS activity, referred to as "parasympathetic tone," that is present, keeping critical systems working well. Without it, the intrinsic nerves within our heart and guts "beat" at their own, slightly faster rhythm. You can think of it in simplistic terms like the gas pedal (SNS) and the brakes (PNS). Our bodies need there to be a continual play between the two. Either a stuck gas pedal or locked-up brakes will lead to a sick, diseased body that ultimately dies. But a balanced interplay of SNS and PNS enables us to react when necessary to something threatening—and then chill out enough to create relationships, reflect on our day and get to sleep. These checks and balances must work together to regulate the critical functions of our bodies.

When the gas pedal gets stuck

Our present-day world tends towards being constantly stimulating. Rather than proper fluctuations between times of threat and times of rest, we tend to live in conditions that favor turning up our sympathetic system and turning down, even overriding, our parasympathetic tone. One aspect of a balanced system and a healthy body (with this fluctuation working well) is that cortisol is secreted in a diurnal fashion: meaning that there are two spikes in a 24 hour period. The first happens around 8 AM and is the larger spike, the second happens around 4 PM and is smaller in amplitude. Cortisol has many actions in the body, impacting blood sugar, immune response, circadian hormonal rhythms. In this twice-daily spike, our body's systems are in balance. But if we sense continued and constant threat, and continued sympathetic drive, cortisol production and secretion are always turned on and lose their diurnal fluctuations. What this means, long-term, is that we damage our bodies' self-modulation, and there is constant activation of the "inflammatory cascade," which we now know leads to heart disease, diabetes, dementia, and autoimmune diseases. It also contributes to the loss of heart rate variability, which increases risk of stroke, cancer—even of dying from any cause (such as getting hit by a bus!).

Information both from our bodies as well as our environment can augment this stress response, making things worse. These internal messages can be "top-down" (including unregulated tv or screen time, constant worrying and anxiety, loss of day/night cycles that go with shift work)—or they can be "bottom-up" (inactivity, eating inflammatory foods like highly processed foods, sugary soda, refined grains). This type of stress creates a constant state of sympathetic over-drive, which leads to very negative consequences over time.

What's going on in your brain?

Deep in our brains on either side lies a small, almond-shaped portion of grey matter called the amygdala. Its job is to scan the environment (the external one via our senses, and the internal one via messages from the vagus nerve and blood-stream). The amygdala causes activation of the SNS when threat is perceived. The amygdala receives neural inputs from our frontal cortex, our storehouse of mem-ory, and our sensory cortices, that actually tell the amygdala what to pay attention to and what to ignore.

Neurobiologists refer to the world that we are capable of perceiving as our "salience map." Being human, with eyes that can perceive depth and bodies that stand upright, leads to some very specific neural connections that determine things we can "see," and that leaves out sensory information that we can't "see" (think of dolphins and bats that echolocate as they navigate the environment, and so have a very different perceptual map of the world). Our salience maps are unique to each person, and evolve depending on the environment each grows up in, with the particular experiences and stimuli that surround us. Facial recogni-tion is a very important skill for infants to learn, for example, and a child's early exposure only to people of the same skin color can lead to difficulty as an adult perceiving nuances of facial characteristics in those of a different skin color. This programming occurs as a result of our anatomy and the conditions in which we are raised. Some of our limitations of perception are "baked in" to the way our nervous system is made (for example, we can't decide to "see" each other with ultrasound waves), and other limitations can be overcome with inten-tional exposure and practice (like seeing the variations of the image of "My Wife and My Mother-in-Law," at the end of Part 1 of this book). Opening ourselves to diverse experiences and perspectives is one way we can begin to expand our salience map.

Arching over the amygdala on each side of the brain is another structure called the hippocampus. Its job is to process and overlay memory on to perceptual ex-periences, attaching to the amygdala's sensory perceptions a story, with nuances of emotions and feeling, and then storing these away so that in the future when a similar threat is presented, these same stories and emotions get activated. Say, for instance, as a child you saw a snake on the ground. Your amygdala sounded the alarm, causing your heart rate to jump, your legs to run away, and you to yell for help. Maybe you were so frightened you even peed your pants. Your hippocampus was busy storing all kinds of additional details and weaving a story...of how scared you were, of your mother's anger at ruining your pants, of shame, maybe even of sensory details that later made sense but maybe weren't things you actually "saw" in the moment. Then, years later as an adult, perhaps you thought you saw a snake, and in the split second that elapsed before you realized it was only a garden hose, the cascade of sympathetic stimulation was already set off, and the story laid down by your hippocampus resurfaced—with all the terror, shame, embarrassment, and sensory detail it stored from years before. Even though you're not actually under attack from a snake, your body acts as though it is, maybe even more strongly than it had during the actual incident when you were a child!

Our salience map is created by many such memories that we have created throughout our life's experience and that continue to impact behavior throughout our life. Many of these are complex and sometimes difficult to engage or work with, if they involve sadness, fear, shame, trauma. The "hamster wheel" of memory, once started, can be quite difficult to get off of. The anatomy of our brain is creating a response based upon the way it is constructed. Attentional practices like meditation and council, however, can encourage us to step back a bit, to see that there is a "gap" between a stimulus and our reactions. This gap can give us enough space to see the difference between our experience and our *story* of our experience, and in that space we can choose a different, more appropriate response based on how we want to navigate the circumstances, rather than a habitual, reflexive reaction that may be colored by old and now inaccurate messages stored in our brains.

In addition to the benefits of attention and mindfulness on modulating our stress response, there are other things we can do intentionally from the "top down," as well as from the "bottom up," that help us recover a healthy autonomic nervous system's cyclicity. Positive influences from the bottom-up include: better nutrition (increasing complex carbohydrates, limiting sugars, favoring vegetables and fresh fruits over processed foods), exercise (particularly, practices that impact the core like yoga and tai chi), and slow, deep breathing. Other positive top-down influences, besides attention and mindfulness, include consciously practicing gratitude and loving kindness towards oneself as well as others.

In fact, gratitude and loving-kindness have been found in studies of the brain (EEG and MRI scans) to be the practices that most quickly cause positive changes in our brains' functioning, as well as actually leading to increased size of portions of the brain that activate during times of empathy towards others. We can actually build a kindness "muscle" through using our brains in certain ways, similar to how one might enlarge one's biceps by doing curls at the gym. And, in terms of the working of our brains, there seems to be no distinction between being kind towards oneself or toward others: practicing kindness and gratitude towards oneself leads to the same positive outcomes as acting kindly towards others (and vice versa).

So, when you are sitting in a council group, your ability to become aware of your own body's physical responses to your surroundings—what is often referred to in council as "reading the field"—gives you information about what's going on inside yourself, in the participants in the circle and in the surroundings. What you then do to take a step back, to cultivate a gap, and to practice modulating your own autonomic response has an impact on yourself and others in the circle. In addition to the benefits discussed above of learning better self-regulation of your autonomic nervous system, this understanding and intentional practice can greatly increase your skills as a council facilitator, minding and sometimes shepherding the flow of council in a group. Consider times you have been with someone who seemed able to remain calm in the midst of turmoil, or times you've been around someone who was agitated beyond explanation, and how it made your body feel. With practices like those described in this book, and developed in council and meditation practice, you can begin to see how modulation of your own reactions has an impact on others. Minding our own self-regulation and balanced stress response enables us to participate more fully and effectively in the group process of council as participant, witness or facilitator.

Council in Schools

(Contributed by Julia Mason Wasson—certified council trainer, writer on education and culture and National Board Certified third grade teacher.)

Why practice council in schools?

Practicing council in classrooms and school communities can help students, as well as educators, build connection. In council, we focus on the words and stories of peers and develop empathy. Council helps children appreciate the diverse backgrounds, experiences, and opinions of their classmates. Being "in council" helps students develop attention, concentration, and listening skills to express themselves fully and appropriately and to suspend preconceptions.

I practiced council in my third—and fourth-grade classroom for over a decade, and as a council trainer, worked with hundreds of teachers and administrators to seed the practice at their schools. Their experiences have contributed a great deal to our understanding of effective methodologies and best practice for implementing council programs in schools.

Many children speak about council as one of the most important things that happens at school. A fourth-grader at Wonderland Avenue Elementary in Los Angeles said, "Council is a time when I can spread my feelings so that people, friends, everyone can understand. I can trust these people, so I have the confidence to share my feelings with them freely. Council helps me face my fears and shyness. I feel very welcomed during any council."

A continuation high school student awaiting the birth of his first child reflects on his three years of council: "Listening to my peers helps me clear up doubts that I have about life. Now that I have a baby who is almost ready to be born, I have learned to listen, speak, and think in a whole new way. I have learned to listen politely and speak maturely without cursing and raising my voice. Through the council experience I have gathered a lot of advice and knowledge, which I think will help me later in life. If you learn to listen, speak, and think from the heart, you will be a peaceful, wise, and better person."

Natalie Plachte White, a high school English teacher, council trainer, and MFT, reflects: "Children or young adults realize that they carry within them hundreds, thousands of stories that belong to them, that make them human. If you want to build a culture of storytelling and empathy, begin with topics that build commonality—your favorite thing about autumn, a moment of joy at school, families. These stories create a hunger to know more. Students learn that their lives yield stories, the same understanding we hope to realize through student writing. Recognizing that stories from their own experiences have value is one of the great yields of council practice."

An administrator, reflecting on how council can help students build caring relationships, notes: "During councils, children can hear stories from the perspective of the bully, the bystander, the target. Our job as educators is to create an environment that helps children hear directly about the experience of classmates, to recognize the pain that is caused, and create the impetus for the brain development that produces empathy."

Council also provides students with experiences that underlie basic literacy. Students learn that their experience matters, that they have stories to tell. They learn that their peers—and their teachers—have diverse life experiences from which we can all learn. When students see that they have a voice, that they have something of value to say, they find pathways to express themselves in writing. When students listen from the heart to the stories of others, and find that they are touched and informed, they will be more likely to transfer this deep listening to their reading, and so more fully comprehend meaning in text.

An often engaging council may accompany exploring a picture book, even with older students, asking students to share about which part sticks with them, why they chose that part, and what connections they see to their own lives. A few books many teachers have used include Faith Ringgold's classic *Tar Beach* (after reading, ask, "Where is your own tar beach?"), Jacqueline Woodson's *The Day You Begin*, Maya Angelou's *Life Doesn't Frighten Me*, and Traci Sorell's *We Are Grateful: Otsaliheliga*. Sharing these stories of everyday life can help students understand that a story need not involve superheroes or outsized adventures to be compelling.

The nature of a council session might vary according to the ages of the students, the character of the group, or any issues that may have arisen on the schoolyard, in the news, or elsewhere. A second-grade council began with everyone sharing a story about a time when they had fun. On another day, students took a silent walk around the campus and then told the varied stories of their journeys. Fourth grade students might share stories about their favorite place at home in order to develop ideas that they will then develop as a memoir. Middle school students shared stories about how social media use impacts them. High schoolers talked about their experiences being undocumented, especially as they planned for life after graduation. Leadership students talked about a leader they admired, and why. In a council dedicated to exploring a conflict, a third-grade student shared a story about a time when she had been unkind to another girl, and how badly she feels thinking back about it. And we are always pleased to see students initiate their own councils in the hallways or on the playground to resolve issues. Wonderland Avenue Elementary students know how to explore conflicts by sharing: *This is what happened. This is what I wanted to happen. This is how I could make things better.*

Council activities can be linked directly to curriculum in academic disciplines. Councils can be used to explore themes in literature, personal connections with historical events in social studies, experiences in scientific observations, reflections on physical activities, and study skills such as time management, prioritizing, and intention setting. Council can also be used for pre-reading and pre-writing activities as well as to review information and to check for understanding.

Councils can involve games, art, singing, tossing bean bags—anything that involves developing student awareness within a group dynamic.

Participating in council has the same benefits for adults in a school community—at staff, committee, teacher/parent, or community meetings. Teachers at my former school found using council helped them model the adult behaviors we wished to encourage in students. Sharing stories amongst staff about their practice, about challenges and successes, transformed the energy on campus. As we prepared to open school for the year, we talked about, "a moment I knew I wanted to become a teacher," "a moment of joy in the classroom," or "a student who sticks in my mind." Teachers became more accountable for speaking and listening during disagreements. We heard from everyone, not just the people who tend to be the most vocal. This feeling permeated even casual interactions: a newer teacher said, "I can walk into anyone's room and ask for something, and get what I need."

If possible, find other educators with whom you can share: a great council you've led or in which you have participated; a time council added something to your class. You might share questions about a time something happened in council that you did not know how to handle, or how to manage issues of discipline, confidentiality, vulnerability, and the incorporation of diverse points of view: *Can we listen without fixing? Can we help students build caring connections to each other? How do we as facilitators develop interpersonal sensitivities that allow us to guide our class?*

Release your own expectations that council will go "deep" or any particular way. Stay in the moment with your students. If you practice regularly, students will have a safe container ready when they need it.

A note about confidentiality

Often, children will teach council practice to their parents so that they can use this tool at home, too. However, personal experiences shared by class members are private. Listening with respect honors that privacy, as does not repeating others' stories outside of the council circle. We tell the students that it is fine to tell people outside the council what the topic was and what you had to say, but it is not okay to tell another person's story. You might use the metaphor of putting feathers back into a pillow, or toothpaste into a tube, to talk about what happens when our agreements about privacy are broken. Students may violate confidentiality agreements; help students self-monitor what they share, and be explicit about how, each time confidentiality is honored, the circle of trust becomes stronger. But when trust is violated, it takes time to rebuild.

Remember, you hold the responsibility to keep the circle safe for everyone. You can ask a student, "Are you sure this is something you feel comfortable sharing?" or suggest, "I'd like to continue this conversation with you outside the circle." Be mindful of your responsibilities, as the adult, to hold safe boundaries, and of your role as a mandated reporter. It occasionally happens that you will hear or learn something that you need to address. For older students, be upfront about your role in keeping students safe. You may need to refer students for services. Know who is available at your site to support your students and families.

Suggestions for getting started

As noted, beginning with the introduction of a council practice for adult staff helps in understanding and integrating council and in navigating personal and professional boundaries. Council can be a great asset in deepening positive school culture, but it is important that it be introduced and embodied by at least some on-site staff before it is offered to students. A council training workshop can be a bonding experience for site staff and a practice which can be engaged in faculty, team or parent meetings, when appropriate, while a subset of staff that have experienced a council workshop may choose to deepen their facilitation skills to offer council to students in class or extracurricular settings. When council is offered to students at school, it's important that teachers and facilitators have access to an adult-only council as a resource for support, to debrief and to grow, not to mention the aforementioned benefits to school culture of an ongoing council for staff.

When introducing council in the classroom, try to have a regular time each week to which students can look forward. Figure out how to form a circle in your classroom. Younger students might make a circle on a rug; older students can help rearrange tables and chairs. Maybe you can form a ring of chairs around the desks, and students inside the ring can bring their chairs.

Invite students to bring talking pieces, objects they're willing to let others hold and that will be safe at school. Or they can bring decorations for the center. Introduce council slowly. Your first councils might only be an opportunity for everyone to make a dedication, share their best moment of the day so far, or a favorite playground activity. You may hear something expressed that will lend itself to a prompt. You might say, "It seems that a few people are thinking about..." or "I connected to hearing someone dedicate the council to...."

To encourage participation, try starting with low-demand prompts or speed rounds—favorite colors or animals, sports figures. Or begin with games, a read-aloud, song, or other activity. Don't feel that you need to explain or introduce all the elements at once. You can bring them in slowly. Include a few moments for students to reflect together on the experience and set intentions for next time.

Supporting the practice

If students are not able to listen respectfully to classmates, it's best not to let the council continue. Remember to share short, authentic stories of your own—your students will love learning more about you, but keep the focus on the students.

It may take many councils for students to get used to being in a circle and to overcome self-consciousness. Go slowly and build good norms. Invite students to reflect about how the circle was for them, and if they might try anything next time to help them focus or to make the circle more effective.

The faculty at Para Los Niños Charter Middle School in Los Angeles came up with the following guidelines for council at their school, to support students who were reticent to engage:

> Allow students to pass, but keep the prompts so engaging that most students will want to share.

> If you find that students are passing a lot, share the prompt ahead of time. Maybe you can find a poem, story, or news article that relates to the topic.

> Invite students ahead of time to make dedications, so they're not on the spot.

> Before going into council with the whole group, give students an opportunity to prepare to tell their story. Use a game, pair/share, speed rounds, or an opportunity to write or draw in response to the prompt *before* sharing with the whole group. A few moments of quiet in which students can make a quick sketch in response to the prompt, and then share their drawing, can invite students who feel less comfortable speaking.

> Provide context. Explain why you chose the prompt. Share your own response. Invite a few volunteers to share ideas, popcorn-style, before passing the talking piece around the circle.

> Keep whiteboards on laps to write out the prompt and use as a visual cue, and/or for students to use to note responses to support their speaking.

> Remind students to hold the talking piece before passing. Try holding the talking piece close to their hearts. Encourage the circle to hold space for those students.

> Use a speed round to get started—for example, a favorite Valentine's candy before a more in-depth round about the holiday.

> Suggest and accept alternative ways to share other than verbal.

> Use check-ins as an opportunity for students to share how they are doing.

Go first to model.

If a student has passed during three councils, speak to them privately and offer some kind of reward for participating verbally. (Remember, passing can be a form of participating.)

Use hip-hop quotations and music students can relate to.

Provide additional opportunities to speak. Allow the piece to go around the circle multiple times.

Coach students on how to build on each other's stories and ideas. Provide stems like "I agree with…," "As someone said…," "That reminds me of…."

In instances where student behavior was distracting, the Paros Los Niños facilitators developed guidelines for supporting students in listening better:

Assign seats. Alternate boys and girls if needed. If you find it takes too much time to move furniture and form a circle, try passing a talking piece from where students are at their seats.

Include a moment of mindfulness or a game before opening, to help students settle.

Remind students that they have silent gestures they can use to show agreement, or that a story resonates.

Let them use special artifacts, like fidget spinners. (Note: For some students, this is an overpowering distraction; use your discretion.)

Encourage all students to share a word or a few words during a witness round to demonstrate active listening.

Provide prompts that students will find fun, engaging, important.

Use every occasion for positive reinforcement: "Great job today pausing with the talking piece," or, "Great job today using a silent signal."

Ask students to reflect on what does or does not make a council successful.

When not in council, refer back to the qualities of speaking or listening that you want to encourage. "Let's listen to Sandra speak just as though we were in council."

As a kindergarten teacher notes, "When we say to children, 'this is a safe place,' children will test it by bringing in the conflict and shadow. They begin to feel, 'this is my place, I belong here.' They will bring in the areas of their lives with which they need help—stresses in their families, the lack of friends, mortality in themselves and the world—all the things over which modern children are stressed, and allowing this material to enter the consciousness of the group is a profound form of respect. For teachers who want to honor their own inner lives and those of students, council is a structured but flexible tool. But it can't be used without the commitment to create a safe container for whatever arises from your group, the building of respect for yourself and your own ability to support children that must come first."

Council Games

(Contributed by Camille Ameen—certified council trainer, actress, arts instructor and nonprofit leader.)

When I first started learning and facilitating council, I was struck with the concept of "initiating in joy." As someone who was not into games, I struggled with the idea of the importance of play. Since those days in the early 1990s, I have turned around my thinking. We understand a lot more about the brain, communication and safety. No one can keep us completely safe. At the same time, if a person enters your council, class, workshop or other space feeling *un*safe, it is very challenging for them to listen.

In addition to inviting a playful and courageous environment for participants, games help us to develop stronger social, emotional, and cognitive learning skills such as self-awareness, self-management, social awareness, empathy, relationship skills, and more responsible decision-making. What follows are some games and activities that help to establish a more non-judgmental (i.e., safer) atmosphere; a creative space for discovery and shared experiences. By using fun, non-competitive, and physically interactive games, we find ourselves laughing *with* rather than *at* one another!

We can "break the ice" by playing games. If we engage our group through this kind of play, people will feel encouraged to explore our connections and vulnerabilities, build bridges as a community, unify the field, and stretch ourselves beyond our comfort zone. And the simple act of physically moving, changing your gaze, etc., can help to shift your energy and state of mind. Games can also be used for the sheer fun of play, which is complete unto itself. They can be a metaphor for life experiences and a great entry point for introducing a prompt for council, including art, movement, theatre, or writing councils. Generally speaking, after finishing an activity, you can ask the group: "Besides having fun, what do you think this game is about?" This can lead to discussions and council prompts.

Most of these activities can be appropriate for diverse populations and any age group with simple adaptations. I have been eager to compile, adapt and share these games, developed over many years by wonderful and generous teachers, and do so with great appreciation and respect.

Ice Breaker and Getting to Know You Games

"Stuffed Animal Toss"

A great first-day activity to build teamwork and support focused, sustained "listening," effective communication, memory... You can use hacky sacks, but they can hurt someone if thrown hard. They are also harder to catch *and* you want to avoid making someone feel uncoordinated. Whatever you use, be sure to get objects that you can put in the washing machine and clean.

1st round—Establish a pattern.

Say your name and something about yourself that you'd like us to know (what you like to do, general likes and dislikes, astrological sign, five "hats" you wear, a hidden talent you have, etc.). You can set the topic or leave it open. Then toss the stuffed animal to someone who hasn't yet received it. Based on the group, they say "Thank you, *(name)*" and then say their own name and something about themselves. Let them know they need to remember *who they received the animal from and who they tossed it to.* Everyone receives the animal once.

2nd round—Same pattern, saying your name and the name of the person you tossed it to.

> Use your judgment about a 2nd prompt—if it took a long time for the first round, just say your name, the name you tossed it to, and toss it to them. If you add a prompt, it could be another thing about yourself, something about your family (number of siblings, where you fit in your family, pets, family habits—eats together, etc.), your cultural background (race, ethnicity, language, food, festivals, music, neighborhood, country of family origin, customs, etc.).

3rd round—Toss animal in silence following the same pattern.

> Whenever appropriate, ask what we need to do to be successful in this? Eye contact? Tossing underhand so it can be caught, rather than throwing it hard at someone? (Like a conversation, if you're "yelling" at a person, they can't hear you/catch the object!) Use your peripheral vision to make sure your animal isn't going to collide with another animal?

4th round—Start adding more animals and see how many they can keep up in the air.

The goal of this round is to keep all the animals in the air. Write down how many animals they were able to keep in the air. The next time you do it, you can challenge them to keep an additional animal in the air.

If the group meets over an extended period of time, you can do the same game, but the first could be something like: my name and a person I admire and why; what I did over Thanksgiving; where I was born; where my ancestors came from; an object or something in nature I value; a favorite food/music/dance from my culture; one thing I like about being who I am (race, ethnicity, skate boarder, etc.); one challenge about being who I am; one thing I admire about someone who is from a different "culture" than me, etc.

Some suggestions for prompts, if you chose to do a follow-up council: What came up for you? Tell a story about a time when there were a lot of distractions; what happened, and how did it affect you? Tell a story about a time when you had "a lot of balls in the air." Tell a story of a time when you "dropped the ball," literally or figuratively. Tell a story of a time you were on the ball or on top of things.

"The Wind Comes and Takes..."

Good for building community, discovering what we have in common, learning new perspectives. This activity is kind of like musical chairs: arrange chairs in a circle with one chair less than the number of people participating. The first person stands in the center and says something that's true about themselves: "The wind comes and takes everyone who..." followed by something that is true about the speaker. Everyone that the statement applies to, must also stand. The person in the center looks around and acknowledges the standing group and then says, "Go!" Everyone standing must change seats and whoever is without a chair stands in the center and repeats the sequence. Remember to let everyone know that there is no pushing or shoving. Also, nobody can sit back in their own seat; if it's a large group, they must move more than one chair over.

Suggested topics the facilitator may offer for the speaker to follow, in order:

1. Simple objects or observable things (everyone who is wearing jeans, has pierced ears, curly hair etc.)

2. Simple likes and dislikes (everyone who likes video games, classical music, soccer, likes to collect coins, everyone who doesn't like spiders, etc.)

3. Family and home stuff (your culture, everyone who has a younger brother, pets, parents who are divorced, etc.)

4. Triumphs you've had or challenges you've faced (everyone who has won an award, lost a family member, struggles with math, etc.)

5. Dreams/hopes/fears/desires/wishes/beliefs

6. Or anything else.

Optional: after playing for a few rounds, add that the person in the center gets to decide, before they say "Go" how everyone must move to get to another chair (everyone must skip, jump on one foot, two feet like a bunny rabbit, moon walk, sideways, like a zombie, twirling around, singing, dancing, etc.)

This activity lends itself to talking about what you did over the week, Spring Break, Thanksgiving, etc. Ideas for prompts in follow-up councils include: What came up for you? What's something you learned about someone else (our group)? Did any themes come up from our responses?

"Take a Stand/Move Forward/Show Up"

This one is great for getting to know each other more deeply, exploring where we are right now. When played live, the group can sit in a circle; when a statement applies to someone, they can stand (if already standing in a circle, they can take a step forward). When played in an online session (via Zoom, for example), it can be done by having participants use the "raise hand" feature, or ask everyone to stop their video and select "hide non-video participants;" when they want to "stand up," they can turn on their video to reappear. If the group is a lot larger than one screen of participants, and you have additional facilitators, use breakout rooms so everyone in the smaller group can easily see who has "shown up."

The facilitator calls out statements for everyone to respond to (which do not have to be true for the facilitator). Participants for whom the statement is true stand up/move forward or, if online, indicate in the chosen fashion. Depending on the group, you can then invite others to make statements that are true about themselves, for others to also respond to (as with "The Wind Comes and Takes"). Some possible questions include "Stand Up/Step Forward/Video on if:"

You've ever had a pet dog/cat (invite them to share name)

You've ever had a pet that's not a dog or cat (invite them to say what kind of pet and its name)

You danced by yourself over the past week (you may want to invite them to show a little of their dancing—and maybe have everyone join in)

You read something that's not news over the last week (you may ask what they read and to share a gem from it)

You play an instrument (if possible, invite them to play a little, if accessible)

You sang over this week (you can invite them to sing a phrase and have everyone repeat it, if they're willing)

You collect things (have them say what they collect and/or show something from their collection, if accessible)

People come to you for assistance (share, if appropriate)

You had an argument or conflict with someone over the last week (share, if appropriate)

You are an optimist (share, if appropriate)

You are expecting something good to happen (share, if appropriate)

When you've developed some trust in the group, you can also use this to explore diversity, culture, prejudice, etc. Some possible council prompts: What came up for you? What's something you learned about someone else (or our group)? Talk about a time when you had something in common with someone that surprised you. Talk about a time when you thought you were the only one who felt a particular way. Talk about a time when you felt you were part of a group or not part of a group.

Imagination and Perspective Games:

"This is a..."

Useful for showing how we all see things differently and the importance of seeing and respecting different seats in the circle; engages the imagination in creative risk taking... When working in-person, use an object (like a loofah on a stick scrub brush, a *big* lollipop, long scarf, clean mop, etc.). With everyone standing in a circle, explain that this *may look* like (for example) a loofah bathing scrubber, etc., but it's actually an earring for a giant—and use or demonstrate it as a dangling earring. The item is passed to the next person, who says "No, that's not an earring for a giant..." (or whatever the previous person had said), "..."it's a fishing rod" (for example), and demonstrate its use as that. Best to let everyone know up front that they have only 5 seconds (for example) to come up with something, and the group should make sure that no one repeats anything that has already been said. Also, whatever they call the actual object, it should have some resemblance to the shape of whatever object you use. And, be sure to let them know it has to be appropriate (if minors, keep it G-rated and avoid objects of violence).

Note: If someone draws a blank, let them know they can present something on the next round. Or, if this is the last round, you'll come back to them before ending. And if there are some who are really into it, you can ask if those who still have ideas want to have a "showdown." If they do, they should take a step towards the center of the circle. This should be a friendly competition!

The online variant for this game requires a bit of adaptation: Ask everyone to have a standard size pen or pencil with them. Set up the order of your "circle." Depending on the population and size of your group, you may want to put people in breakout rooms of 7–12 people. Let participants know the order of the circle—a volunteer can write out everyone's names and read out the order. If people don't know each other, you can begin with introductions (name, where they're joining from, one thing they're grateful for, or something else to share). If using breakout rooms, a good rule of thumb for time-frame is approximately ten minutes for seven participants (add a minute for each person over seven). Instructions should be repeated and time shown in an onscreen timer, if possible.

To begin, the facilitator shows their pen/pencil and says: "This may look like a pencil/pen, but it's actually a Q-tip/Stick shift for a sports car/magic wand/etc." Demonstrate it in action based on whatever you identified it as. Pass it to the next person in the circle's predetermined order—who receives it and says: "No, that's not a _____, it's a _____," demonstrating both uses. The game progresses as in the above.

After playing, consider a council about how we all see things differently and that there isn't always a "right" answer; seeing things differently can be an opportunity for us to expand our perspective, and ability to understand one another better. Some prompt ideas: Tell a story about a time when you changed your mind about somebody. Tell a story about a time when you disagreed with someone and how you dealt with it. Tell a story about a time when you heard/saw something and it changed your perspective. Tell a story about a time when you stereotyped someone, or you saw someone else stereotype someone. What happened? Tell a story about a time when you were with somebody very different from you.

"Fortunately—Unfortunately"

This is a game that stimulates the imagination, helps and challenges people to see different perspectives (the good as well as the unfortunate), focuses listening, and reinforces collaboration and building on each other's ideas.

If playing in-person, stand or sit in a circle. If online, depending on the population and size of your group, you may want to put people in breakout rooms of about 7–10, or divide your group in half and have one half go around while the other half is an audience, and then switch.

One person begins a story with "Fortunately..." or "Unfortunately..." and introduces our main character (name, age, location, what's happening, and anything else they want to say). The story can be about any kind of character (human, animal, plant, magical, an object that talks, etc). When the first person finishes, the next person builds onto what the first person said, but from the perspective of the opposite word. If the first person started the story with "Fortunately..." the next person would start the next piece with "Unfortunately...." Everyone gets up to 3 sentences to contribute to the story.

Here's an example:

> 1st person: "*Fortunately*, Daisy woke up to a beautiful day. She ran to the

window and saw the sun shining brightly. Daisy thought, this is the perfect day for my 9th birthday party!"

Next person: "*Unfortunately*, about an hour later, Daisy saw that there was a huge thunderhead cloud right over her house. Suddenly, with a giant bolt of lightning, it began raining cats and dogs! Her mother said, 'Oh, no, what a mess for your birthday party!'"

Next person: "But, *fortunately*, Daisy loved cats and dogs, so she ran outside to play with them all."

Next person: "*Unfortunately*..." and so on.

Continue around the group by alternating back and forth between "*Fortunately*" and "*Unfortunately*" until the story reaches a conclusion or the facilitator decides to end.

Note: You can choose to end the story with the last person in your group, or go around twice. If you have time, you could do a second story—maybe make it magical, a mystery, an adventure, a particular genre, etc. Start with another person who begins with the opposite word from their first round. Be funny, silly, dramatic... anything you want.

(The children's book *Fortunately*, by Remy Charlip, might be something you want to read before playing the game for younger participants.)

If you want to follow this game with a council, some suggestions for prompts include:

Share a story about a time you thought you were "stuck," and what happened. Tell of a time when you helped someone else who thought they were "stuck" and what happened. Talk about a time you had an obstacle in your way. Talk about a time you thought everything was going great, or not great, and what happened.

Note: For those interested in additional games and activities suitable for council sessions, Camille has compiled a booklet, available by contacting her directly at muscletn@wgn.net.

Selected Resources for Further Reading

Baldwin, Christina. 1998. *Calling the Circle: The First and Future Culture.* Bantam Doubleday Dell Publishers.

Baldwin, Christina. 2010. *The Circle Way: A Leader in Every Chair.* Berrett-Koehler Publishers.

Baldwin, Christina. 2005. *Songcatcher: Making Sense of Our Lives Through the Power and Practice of Story.* New World Library.

Bays, Jan Chozen. 2014. *Mindfulness on the Go.* Shambhala Publications.

Brady, Mark. (Ed.). 2003. *The Wisdom of Listening.* Wisdom Publications.

Brown, Brené. 2015. *Daring Greatly: How the Courage to Be Vulnerable Transforms the Way We Live, Love, Parent, and Lead.* Avery.

Boal, Augusto. 2002. *Games for Actors and Non-Actors.* Routledge.

Boyes-Watson, Carolyn. 2008. *Peacemaking Circles and Urban Youth.* Living Justice Press.

Buhner, Stephen Harold. 2004. *The Secret Teachings of Plants.* Bear and Company.

Cahill, Sedonia & Halpern, Joshua. 1990. *The Ceremonial Circle: Practice, Ritual, and Renewal for Personal and Community Healing.* HarperCollins.

Campbell, Joseph. 2008. *The Hero with A Thousand Faces.* New World Library.

Coyle, Daniel. 2018. *The Culture Code.* Bantam.

Forest, Ohky Simine. 2009. *Dreaming the Council Ways: True Native Teachings from the Red Lodge.* Red Wheel/Weiser.

Foster, Steven. 1989. *Book of Vision Quest: Personal Transformation in Wilderness.* Touchstone Books.

Foster, Steven & Little, Meredith. 1989. *The Roaring of the Sacred River.* Simon & Schuster.

Glassman, Bernie. 1998. *Bearing Witness: A Zen Master's Lessons in Making Peace.* Bell Tower.

Goleman, Daniel. 1995. *Emotional Intelligence.* Bantam Books.

Graveline, Fyre Jean. 1998. *Circle Works: Transforming Eurocentric Consciousness.* Fernwood Publishing.

Greenland, Susan Kaiser. 2010. *The Mindful Child.* Atria Books.

Halifax, Joan. 2004. *The Fruitful Darkness.* Grove Press.

Halifax, Joan. 1979. *Shamanic Voices.* EP Dutton.

Halifax, Joan. 2018. *Standing at the Edge.* Flatiron Books.

Huang, Chungliang Al & Lynch, Jerry. 1995. *Mentoring, The Tao of Giving and Receiving Wisdom.* HarperOne.

Johnson, Robert. 1994. *Owning Your Own Shadow.* HarperSanFrancisco.

Johnson, Robert. 2001. *Emergence: The Connected Lives of Ants, Brains, Cities and Software*. Scribner.

Kessler, Rachael. 2000. *The Soul of Education: Helping Students Find Connection, Compassion, and Character at School*. Association for Supervision and Curriculum Development.

Macy, Joanna. 1998. *Coming Back to Life: Practices to Reconnect Our Lives, Our World*. New Society Publishers.

Macy, Joanna, Seed, John & Fleming, Pat. 2007. *Thinking Like a Mountain: Towards a Council of All Beings*. New Catalyst Books.

Mattis-Namgyel, Elizabeth. 2011. *The Power of an Open Question*. Shambhala.

Mille Bojer, Marianne, Roehl, Heiko, Knuth, Marianne & Magner, Collen. 2012. *Mapping Dialogue: Essential Tools for Social Change*. Taos Institute Publications.

Murdock, Maureen. 1987. *Spinning Inward: Using Guided Imagery with Children for Learning, Creativity, & Relaxation*. Shambhala Publications.

Murthy, Vivek H. 2020. *Together: The Healing Power of Human Connection in a Sometimes Lonely World*. Harper Wave.

Peck, M. Scott. 1987. *The Different Drum: Community Making and Peace*. Touchstone.

Plotkin, Bill. 2007. *Nature and the Human Soul: Cultivating Wholeness and Community in a Fragmented World*. New World Library.

Pranis, Kay. 2005. *The Little Book of Circle Processes, A New/Old Approach to Peacemaking*. Little Books of Justice & Peacebuilding.

Pranis, Kay; Stuart, Barry & Wedge, Mark. 2003. *Peacemaking Circles: From Crime to Community*. Living Justice Press.

Ross, Rupert. 1996. *Returning to the Teachings: Exploring Aboriginal Justice*. Penguin Books.

Scharmer, Otto. 2013. *Leading from the Emerging Future*. Berrett-Koehler Publishers.

Scharmer, C. Otto, Jaworski, Joseph, & Flowers, Betty Sue. 2004. *Presence.* Doubleday.

Senge, Peter, et al. 2018. *Presence.* Currency.

Spolin, Viola. 1986. *Theatre Games for the Classroom.* Northwestern University Press.

Zehr, Howard. 2015. *The Little Book of Restorative Justice.* Good Books.

Zimmerman, Jack & Coyle, Virginia. 2009. *The Way of Council.* Bramble Books.

Zimmerman, Jack & McCandless, Jaquelyn. 1998. *Flesh and Spirit.* Bramble Books.

And the poems of Wendell Berry, Hafiz, Mary Oliver,
Rainer Maria Rilke, Jelaluddin Rumi, William Stafford,
Derek Walcott, and David Whyte

ABOUT THE AUTHOR

Jared Seide is the Executive Director of Center for Council (centerforcouncil.org), a nonprofit organization that trains practitioners in mindfulness and council to promote wellness and resiliency, foster compassion and build community. Seide has worked extensively with schools, healthcare organizations, elder care facilities, prisons, law enforcement organizations, community based organizations and businesses to promote individual wellness and resilience and to foster thriving organizations and communities.

Seide has developed and shepherded: *Peace Officer Wellness, Empathy & Resiliency Training* to promote health, relationality and compassion amongst police and correctional officers; *Compassion, Attunement & Resilience Education for Healthcare Professionals*, focusing on burnout and dysregulation amongst physicians, nurses and other first responders; *Council for Insight, Compassion & Resilience*, an award-winning transformational insight and accountability-oriented rehabilitation program for incarcerated populations; the *Organizational Wellness Project*, to help build positive organizational culture within public and private companies; as well as other council-based programs to support and resource impacted communities and emerging leaders.

Seide has led trainings and retreats focusing on compassion, reconciliation and community-building throughout the U.S., as well as in Poland, Rwanda, France, Colombia and Bosnia-Herzegovina. He has led workshops, presentations and conference seminars around the world and has been a Resident Fellow at the Rockefeller Foundation's Bellagio Center. Seide is a graduate of Brown University and the chaplaincy program of the Upaya Institute.

Made in the USA
Monee, IL
30 August 2023

41849236R00149